Wild about Cornwall

David Chapman

Alison Hodge

Dedication

Now I know why authors
dedicate books to people!

To my wife, Sarah.
Thank you for your confidence
and support.

Acknowledgements

I am indebted to all of the site managers and wardens of the reserves detailed in this book. Without their lucid explanations of management strategies and knowledge of species prospering in their care, none of this would have been possible.

On a broader note, we should all be grateful to the conservation groups working to maintain their parts of Cornwall in such a beautiful, vibrant and healthy condition. Charities such as the Cornwall Wildlife Trust, RSPB and the National Trust can only continue this work if supported by us.

David Chapman

Published in 2007 by
Alison Hodge
Bosulval, Newmill, Penzance, Cornwall TR20 8XA
info@alison-hodge.co.uk www.alison-hodge.co.uk

© David Chapman 2007
This edition © Alison Hodge 2007

ISBN 978-0-906720-51-6

British Library Cataloguing-in-Publication Data
A catalogue record for this book is available from the British Library.

Designed and originated by BDP –
Book Development and Production,
Penzance, Cornwall

Printed in China on paper produced with elemental chlorine-free pulp, harvested from managed sustainable forests.

Introduction

Cornwall has changed my life. Its places; its people; its communities; its environment; its history, and its wildlife are all so deeply intertwined that they create a blend of unparalleled county loyalty, belonging and passion. My own involvement in this mix has always been most strongly rooted in the world of nature – and what a rich tapestry of natural wonders this county has to offer.

The processes involved in the creation of what we see today have been in operation for around 500 million years. With the underlying geology of the county completed about 300 million years ago, geographical processes have since shaped, and continued to reshape, the landscape. Most recently, the impact of our own hand can be witnessed in a huge variety of ways, often with extraordinary effect.

Geological forces were responsible for the intrusions of granite which created the rich supply of minerals that once brought prosperity to the county. The same forces gave us the two-tone slates so obvious on the north Cornwall coast; the folds which have later appeared in them, and the rock pools, such as those at Polzeath, in which we can now delve for marine life. The underlying rocks are responsible for the mineral content of the soil, and this is often critical in determining the vegetation that we see on the surface. Nowhere is this connection more accurately made than on the Lizard, where we have a unique range of flowers growing on the magnesium-rich soils created by serpentine.

The varied geology creates differing levels of resistance to erosion, and the many obvious landscape forms, such as Kit Hill in the east and Godolphin Hill in the west, that we see today. Around the coast and on the land are a variety of features created by a combination of geology and geomorphology. Wonderfully shaped headlands, such as that of Gurnard's Head, provide a canvas on which nature creates its colourful paintings. Sea stacks and arches, carved by the erosive effects of the ocean from 400-million-year-old rocks along the north coast of Cornwall, like those at Basset's Cove near Tehidy, stand as an epitaph to the forces of nature. Granite sculptures on tors and sea cliffs, including the magnificent examples found on the Isles of Scilly and at Porthgwarra, create a feeling of awe and inspiration.

Climate has played its role in the process of landscape formation. Varying global temperatures have changed sea levels repeatedly, and examples of their effect can be seen at Loe Bar where a barrier beach has been formed; at Cot Valley where strata in the cliff stand testament to an incredible cycle of events, and around the Fal Estuary where rising sea levels caused the flooding of river valleys to create the characteristic rias with overhanging oak trees, such as those near Tresillian. The current temperate climate combined with geographical position provides us with an environment in which the Dartford warbler – a bird more typical of the Mediterranean region, but which is resident on Goss Moor and Kit Hill – can survive in the same county as the spring sandwort – a flower associated with Arctic tundra, but which can be found growing on the Lizard.

The county's geographical position has a profound impact on its weather and natural phenomena. Salt-laden wind is a regular feature, and this is responsible for the stunted, gnarled and bent trees of our coast and moors. It also brings with it the clean Atlantic air which encourages luxuriant growth in our lichens and mosses, including fine examples at the National Nature Reserve of Golitha Falls on the edge of Bodmin Moor. The rain comes in heavy doses, but it creates a lushness of growth in our hedgerows and woodlands that is the envy of the world: we need look no further than the bluebell woods at Lanhydrock and Antony for evidence of this. Each year we are visited by birds from all over the world. The shape of our peninsula funnels migrants from the east, and our headlands provide sanctuary to wind-blown vagrants from the west. During the autumn, in the coastal valleys of West Penwith, we can see warblers from Asia sitting alongside thrushes from North America and flycatchers from Scandinavia.

The effect of our own hand is tempered by time through nature's processes, but we began seriously influencing the environment many thousands of years ago. Our inland heaths, such as those at Goonhilly, would once have been forested, but are now home to a colourful array of heathers and insects. More recent agriculture has created some of our most astonishing spectacles, including the poppies and corn marigolds of West Pentire, and the purple viper's bugloss of Boscregan.

The most obvious effect of our hand on the environment in Cornwall is that of the mining industry. The processes of nature are yet to reclaim much of the areas worst affected during this era, partly because of the relative recentness, but also because of the nature of the waste left behind. Engine houses still stand; buddles still hold water, and mining waste still resists the growth of many plants; but lichens thrive; thrift flourishes, and bats such as the rare greater horseshoe treat the old shafts as they would a natural cave. The mining was not restricted to taking rocks from deep holes in the ground; a great deal of the work was carried out in streams. Tin-streaming has recreated entire landscapes, such as the Bissoe Valley, where we can now enjoy a reserve established for dragonflies in a valley once exploited for its minerals.

The mining industry brought with it a whole host of peripheral industries, many of which are now protected in our nature reserves. The gunpowder works of Kennall Vale, and the dynamite factory on Upton Towans are classic examples. The shape and size of the trees in our woodlands, which might seem untouched by our hand, are in fact a consequence of our industrial heritage. Almost all of our woods have been coppiced for hundreds of years to produce charcoal and timber for the mining industry.

Historically, we may have taken the environment for granted, but our actions have sometimes inadvertently created unusual havens in which different species of wildlife could make a home. After a downturn in the fortunes of our natural history in the second half of the twentieth century, we are the generation responsible for maintaining and improving the great diversity which Cornwall offers.

If we allow nature to simply take its course, then many of the habitats that we have created will revert to woodland. The consensus among conservationists is to try to conserve the best in each habitat that we currently have. To this end we can now witness rare breeds of livestock on our coast to encourage spring flowers, and the woodlands in our nature reserves are being coppiced so that butterflies such as the pearl-bordered fritillary can continue to live in the Marsland Valley, and dormice can thrive at Cabilla.

If, at the beginning of the twenty-first century, you need a sign to show that the health of the environment is improving, you need look no further than the story of the chough highlighted in Site 22, Kynance to Lizard. Here we have the return of a prodigy to the county where it belongs.

David Chapman
March 2007

Contents

Loe Bar.

Foreword

I have always felt extremely fortunate to have been born in Cornwall, and to have lived in the county for most of my life. It is a very special place that is cherished by residents and visitors alike.

A key reason for this love of Cornwall is its varied landscape and wildlife-rich natural environment, coupled with a unique historic and cultural heritage. These features make it an area full of interest and inspiration – simply a great place to live or visit.

In this book David brings to life through words and photographs a marvellous selection of the jewels in the crown of Cornwall's natural environment. I am sure it will encourage readers to explore wild Cornwall, visit areas new to them, or look more closely at familiar haunts, armed with the additional information provided. In turn I hope this book will do much to foster an appreciation of our natural heritage, and a determination to safeguard it for future generations.

Read, enjoy, explore, and encourage your family and friends to do likewise.

Trevor Edwards
Chief Executive
Cornwall Wildlife Trust

How to Use This Book

Wild about Cornwall is a celebration of the natural history of Cornwall. It aims to encourage a greater appreciation of the very best places to see its flora and fauna, in a variety of habitats across the county. The choice of 40 sites is a personal one. They are organized in an approximately anticlockwise direction, starting from the north.

The descriptions of each site convey something of the spirit of the location, as well as practical details about how to find your way around, or where to go for the best wildlife. It is intended that this book should be used in conjunction with an Ordnance Survey map when planning a trip to a location. Distances are given in miles; other measurements are in metric, except for historical data. Species are referred to by their most frequently used common names.

At the end of each site is a box entitled 'Look out for', which highlights the wildlife that can be seen through the year. This may repeat species mentioned in the text, but is viewable at a glance.

At the back of the book are sections that will help you to plan a visit, with details of optimum months for every location, and optimum locations for every month. Also given here are contact details for various organizations, and a complete index of around 580 species mentioned in the book, with their scientific names.

Every effort has been made to ensure that the details provided in *Wild about Cornwall* are accurate at the time of writing. If you have any comments regarding the book, or would like to see more of my photography, then please visit my website at www.davidchapman.org.uk.

Key to Checklists

In the checklists can be found the following:
- *Number of site.*
- *Type of location* – usually a nature reserve or a walk along public rights of way.
- *Map* – the number of the OS *Explorer* 1:25 000 (two and a half inches to the mile); OS *Landranger* 1:50 000 (one inch to the mile), or OS *Outdoor Leisure* 1:25 000 map on which the location can be found.
- *Directions to start point* – directions by road to the place where a car can be parked.
- *Start point* – the grid reference of the start of the walk or the entrance to the reserve.
- *Size* – if the location is a nature reserve.
- *Length* – the approximate length of the walk in miles [ml] if the location involves a set walk. Where no length is given, the site can be explored freely.
- *Recommended time* – length of a visit, allowing plenty of time to look for wildlife.
- *Conditions* – an impression of conditions underfoot.
- *Habitats* – the types of habitat found on site.
- *Points of interest* – the map reference for specific points mentioned in the text, to help plan a route.
- *Landscape designation* – AGLV (Area of Great Landscape Value); AONB (Area of Outstanding Natural Beauty); LNR (Local Nature Reserve); NNR (National Nature Reserve); RIGS (Regionally Important Geological Site); SAC (Special Area of Conservation); SSSI (Site of Special Scientific Interest).
- *Owner* – name, if relevant. Contact details are given here or on page 249.
- *Open* – when site is open for access, if relevant.
- *Entry* – states whether access is free or charged.
- *Enquiries* – contact telephone number.
- *Nearest facilities* – where there are none on site, the nearest village or town where basic facilities can be found. (Not listed if facilities on site.)
- *Site facilities* – see the key to symbols used in the book inside the front cover.

site number	**1**
type of location	**Nature reserve**
map	*Explorer* 126; *Landranger* 190
directions to start point	**By road: Turn L off A39 (Bude to Hartland) at Crimp. After 2 ml turn R towards Gooseham; turn L just before riding stables; turn R at T-junction; after 0.5 ml road bends L; limited parking on the track to R. (Alternative parking at Welcombe Mouth, SS 214 180, but access is along a narrow rough track.)**
starting point	**SS 217 170**
size	**212 ha/524 a**
length	**Up to 4 ml**
recommended time	**Up to 3 hours**
conditions	**Rocky and muddy**
habitats	**Woodland, cliff, rocky beach, river, scrub, farmland**
points of interest	**Gooseham Mill SS 232 172; Welcombe Mouth SS 214 180; Marsland Mouth SS 212 173**
landscape designation	**AONB, LNR, SAC, SSSI**
owner	**CWT and DWT**
open	**All year**
entry	**Free**
enquiries	**T: 01872 273 939 (CWT)**
nearest facilities	**Kilkhampton**
site facilities	

Welcombe and Marsland

The valleys of Marsland and Welcombe sink deep into the coastal landscape of North Cornwall. Situated on, and extending over, the border with Devon this delightful area is home to a wide range of wildlife, and offers exhilarating cliff-top walking combined with more sheltered and secluded wooded valleys.

The variety of habitats in and around these valleys, and their potential to provide for wildlife, was first recognized by Christopher Cadbury. His family's interest in confectionary and religion is well known, but Christopher was also a keen and highly respected conservationist who purchased land around the world in a bid to protect it for future generations to enjoy. In the 1960s he bought much of the land around the Welcombe and Marsland valleys, and at around the same time became president of the Royal Society for Nature Conservation – a position he held until 1988. The reserve is now managed jointly by the Wildlife Trusts of Cornwall and Devon.

Into the sea flow the two rivers responsible for creating much of the landscape that we see here today. It is hard to imagine how these relatively small rivers carved out such deep and craggy valleys, but the combination of erosion and gravity over a period of time have worked to great effect. Standing at the edge of the steep-sided Marsland Valley looking out over sea, river, coastal heath and woodland is certainly a rewarding experience.

In an attempt to divide the area into habitats I will start on the beaches of either valley. Not your typical bucket-and-spade beach, this is a unique look at the

The Marsland Water flows through the heavily wooded valley.

effects of the last 320 million years of rock formation and alteration. The land here was once firmly under water, and the sediments that now form the rocks were being deposited by the sea as alternating layers of mud and sand. Over time, pressure caused the sediments to harden, creating bands of rock of differing strength. Uneven pressure and earth movements folded the rocks at will before the sea level began to rise again. Now we see the effects of wave erosion on these contorted strata, with layers roughly sliced off by the power of the ocean.

The rock pools trapped by these roughly linear strata are worth a delve, and rising up from the beach are craggy cliffs that are home to nesting seabirds such as fulmars, shags and guillemots. Fulmars, which nest on the cliffs, look a little like gulls but fly on stiff, straight wings, more often gliding than flapping. They use the wind and up-draughts of air around the cliffs to keep them buoyant, but still have trouble landing on their rocky ledges. Look closely at these birds and you will see they have nostril tubes, allowing the fulmar to secrete extremely salty water, and so to drink and purify seawater. The name fulmar derives from the two words *foul* and *maa*. *Maa* is the old word for gull, which is not very accurate since this bird is related to the petrel family, but the *foul* is entirely appropriate since the fulmar has an unusual defensive mechanism which consists of throwing up on predators. The oily, fishy vomit is not only offensive, but it can clog up birds' feathers leaving them immobile.

On the landward side of the cliffs is an area of coastal heath. Dominated by gorse and heather, this

Left: Fulmars nest on the coast.
Right: Primroses flourish in the coppiced woodland (top). Dog violets are encouraged since they are the food plant of the fritillary's caterpillars (bottom left). Wood sorrel is extremely numerous in the Marsland Valley (bottom right).

Left: The obvious silvery spot in the middle of the pearl-bordered fritillary's under-wing is diagnostic.
Right: The small pearl-bordered fritillary has more pale spots on its under-wing.

habitat is a blaze of colour at most times of the year. Adding to the variety of flora is a wide range of spring and summer flowers, including wild carrot, thrift and sea campion. Pausing to call from the highest spikes of vegetation a stonechat may welcome visitors into its domain, while a passing raven occasionally croaks nonchalantly as it flies purposefully overhead.

In the depths of the Marsland Valley the sound of breaking waves gives way to water cascading over rapids in the streams. The noisy 'chissick' of a pied or grey wagtail may distract momentarily, but the sound of the river is continual.

The footpath from the suggested car-parking area leads into the Marsland Valley, which is the more productive of the two valleys, though the walk over the coast path into Welcombe Valley is also rewarding. On entering the reserve an interpretation panel gives a possible route. The gentle descent along the rocky track from the car-park passes through a delightfully mixed woodland of oak, ash, holly, rowan, beech, hazel and sycamore. Alongside this path, in spring, the flowers are tremendous. The usual range of woodland flowers is present, but for me the density of wood sorrel in late March is fantastic.

One of the most valuable sections of the reserve is on the south-facing, wooded slope of the Marsland Valley towards Gooseham Mill. Here the trees are coppiced to create clearings, and vegetation is mown or grazed to keep it in check so that flowers and insects can flourish. The key species is the extremely rare pearl-bordered fritillary, found at only a few sites in Cornwall, but the similar, small pearl-bordered fritillary also occurs here, creating a potential problem of identification.

The pearl-bordered fritillary tends to fly a little earlier than the small pearl-bordered, peaking in May instead of June, but there is an overlap, so for a positive identification a detailed look at the butterfly is necessary. From the upper side the two species can look identical, so the easiest way to separate them is by looking at the underside of the hind wing, which is visible when the butterfly is at rest. The pearl-bordered fritillary has an obvious, isolated silver spot in the centre of this wing, which is not as obvious in the small pearl-bordered fritillary because its whole under-wing is much paler. It is also on the under-wing that both species have the seven white spots or 'pearls' along the outer edge, from which they get their name.

Like many other fritillaries the pearl-bordered fritillary lays its eggs on the leaves of dog violets – a flower which grows best in woodland clearings. The Wildlife Trust manages the woodland here with great sensitivity to the needs of both the violet and the butterfly.

Ideal conditions include not only plenty of violets, but also a covering of bracken. The bracken serves to shade the violets from the burning sun during the hot summer months, and in the early spring, when the butterflies emerge, the dead bracken provides a microclimate of shelter and warmth at ground level.

Ideal conditions for the emergence of these butterflies seem to include a largely settled warm period, with a little dampness to help soften the pupae just before they finally break out.

LOOK OUT FOR

April–May: Flowers in the woods include bluebells, wood sorrel, lesser celandine, wood anemone and primrose. On the coast there is thrift, sea campion and spring squill.

Late April–early May: Peak time for emergence of the very rare pearl-bordered fritillary.

Late May–June: Peak time for emerging small pearl-bordered fritillaries.

Summer: A good time for rock-pooling. Keep an eye out to sea for a pod of bottlenose dolphins. Families of stonechats chatter from the tops of gorse; male whitethroats sing out their scratchy song from similar terrain. Fulmars nest on the cliffs, and you may see guillemots here.

September–October: Look for migrating birds along the coast and in the shelter of the valleys.

All year: Raven, buzzard, kestrel, sparrowhawk and peregrine can all be seen soaring overhead. Some summer migrants never leave the shelter of the valley. Blackcaps and chiffchaffs are two species that over-winter here.

2

Walk on public rights of way

Explorer 111; *Landranger* 190

By road: From A39 follow signs to Bude. Park by quay

SS 207 062

4 ml (return from Bude to Helebridge)

3 hours

Level ground, towpath

Canal, woodland, fields

LNR overlooking Petherick's Mill Marsh SS 209 055; Weir SS 214 038; Helebridge Wharf SS 216 037. Permitted path to coast leaves canal at SS 213 044, joins coast path at SS 201 042

AGLV, LNR, SAC, SSSI

NCDC

All year

Free

T: 01208 265 644 (NCDC)

The Bude Canal

For the builders of the Bude Canal, I am sure that helping wildlife was the last thing on the agenda. But inadvertently, and with the mellowing of time, a wildlife paradise has been formed.

The Bude Canal was conceived in the eighteenth century, but its construction did not start until 1819 using prisoners taken during the Napoleonic war. The entire 35½ miles of canal, including the dam at the Lower Tamar Lake, an aqueduct, three conventional locks and six inclined planes, were constructed in six years – an amazing feat when you consider the kind of work involved.

The purpose of the canal was to transport sand, which, because of its high shell content, was used as a fertilizer on inland farms. To collect the sand, railway lines were laid out across the beach, and a small turntable, still visible today, was used to switch trucks from these tracks on to a single line running alongside the quay. The sand was then tipped from these small railway trucks into boats on the canal.

Inclined planes were constructed instead of the vast number of locks that would have been required to lift the boats to a height of 433 feet above sea level. The slopes were incorporated into the system by fitting boats with wheels to enable them to be pulled up rails. Most of the inclined planes had waterwheels to power the lifting mechanism but one, at Hobbacott, was operated using a bucket and well system.

Frequent accidents, such as the snapping of chains and the breaking of axles, caused regular delays, and the canal company didn't once make an annual profit. Its poor financial state, together with competition from the railway line in the 1870s, caused the canal to begin the process of closing down, and by 1891 it had ceased trading completely.

The Bude Canal offers great tranquillity.

Mute swans can usually be found around the canal basin in Bude.

Since that time nature has taken the upper hand. One reason why this area is so rich in wildlife is that the stretch of canal that remains intact runs alongside the River Neet in its floodplain. The land between the two is relatively undisturbed, and offers a great deal of cover in the form of reed and iris beds. The floodplain is now valued by locals not only as a nature reserve, but also because it acts as a flood defence for their town. So good is this particular spot for birds that it has been designated a Local Nature Reserve (LNR), and the natural flooding of the river helps to create a wetland suitable for ducks and waders, particularly in winter.

The canal is well stocked with fish, and their activity does not go unnoticed. Apart from the human anglers, grey herons and kingfishers regularly prowl this stretch of canal. Otters are present in both the river and the canal, but are seldom seen since there is so much thick cover into which they can disappear. The other mammal which I would love to be able to

Mallards raise their young along the canal.

say lives here is the water vole, but unfortunately, despite frequent rather hopeful records, it seems that Ratty is no longer alive in Cornwall, though it is likely that this was its last stand in the county.

Early summer is a good time to walk the canal. Swallows and house martins hunt for food low over the surface of the water, and land on the wet margins of river and canal to collect mud with which to make their nests. Swinging in the breeze at the top of the reed stems, sedge and reed warblers can be heard singing to proclaim their territories. Slightly less bold in song, but perhaps more attractive in appearance, are the reed buntings which are also numerous here. The contrast between the male's black head and white belly make him an easy bird to identify. But the reed bunting became a much rarer sight in the countryside during the last quarter of the twentieth century.

In winter the wetland between the canal and river plays host to a completely different set of birds. Dampened by the rains of autumn, the area becomes

Left: The teal is a common winter visitor to the marshes between the canal and the river.
Above: Sedge warblers are summer visitors to the reed-beds along the canal.

Around the weir connecting the river and canal is a stretch of woodland offering a more sheltered environment. Here there are beautiful demoiselles around the canal's edge: this type of damselfly lives around slowly moving water, unlike most of its kind which prefer a static medium. Compared with other damselflies this is quite a large species, with a very graceful flight reminiscent of a butterfly. Both males and females are colourful and iridescent – the males blue, the females green. Like all damselflies the beautiful demoiselle rests with its wings held back alongside its body, in contrast to the dragonflies which hold their wings out.

Across the A30 is Helebridge Wharf. This expanse of still water is now used as a stocking pool for fish, and the overhanging trees create a calm and attractive environment. Comfrey grows in profusion along the edges of the lake, where the indiscriminate mower cannot reach, its rich purple flowers hanging in clusters among its furry foliage. This plant has been used for many different purposes down the

attractive to waders and wildfowl. Waders such as lapwing, curlew, snipe and golden plover can be numerous here, and ducks usually include wigeon and teal. This is also the best time of year to see king-fishers, since many fly downstream to more coastal areas to spend the winter in slightly milder climes.

Left: A male beautiful demoiselle on purple loosestrife.
Right: A bee is attracted to comfrey growing around the canal at Helebridge.

years: the leaves eaten in a similar way to spinach; the roots used to make plaster to set bones, and as a medicine for a wide variety of ailments. Adjacent to the wharf is the Barge Workshop, which contains the only surviving tub boat from the canal. No doubt there are many more in the mud!

To walk the Bude Canal, park either in Bude or in the small car-park at Helebridge Wharf. If starting from Bude, a circular route can be made by taking the permitted path through community woodland to return along the coast path.

LOOK OUT FOR

April–May: Warblers include reed, sedge, willow, whitethroat, blackcap and chiffchaff. On the wetland look out for whimbrel, black-tailed godwits, and other waders on migration. The cattle pasture alongside the canal might be a good spot for yellow wagtails on migration; cuckoos can often be heard.

June–September: Dragonflies and damselflies abound; flag iris, meadowsweet, water-lily, valerian, hemlock water dropwort, bulrush and purple loosestrife all flower in or on the canal and river. Mute swans, moorhens, coots, mallards and Canada geese nest in the adjacent area, and all have young in June and July. The rough grazing areas are a prime hunting ground for barn owls: look for them at dusk.

July–September: Green and common sandpiper on Petherick's Mill Marsh.

Autumn–Winter: Waders such as lapwing, curlew, snipe, golden plover; wildfowl, particularly wigeon and teal, on wetland areas.

All year: Possibly kingfisher, grey heron.

type of location	Walk on public rights of way
map	*Explorer* 111; *Landranger* 190, 200
directions to start point	By road: From A39 N of Wadebridge follows signs to Boscastle
starting point	SX 100 914
length	Coastal walk S to Tintagel one way approx 6 ml
recommended time	4 hours (to walk one way from Boscastle to Tintagel)
conditions	Difficult, steep and rocky
habitats	Cliffs, woodland, river valley, arable fields, coastal heath
points of interest	Willapark Iron Age Cliff Castle SX 091 913; Forrabury Stitches SX 094 912; cliff grazing scheme SX 100 918; California Quarry SX 091 909; Rocky Valley SX 073 895; Short Island SX 077 908; The Sisters SX 061 900; County Council Visitor Centre, Boscastle, SX 100 913, T: 01840 250 010
landscape designation	AONB, RIGS, SAC, SSSI
owner	NT owns much of the land
entry	Free
enquiries	T: 01208 742 81 (NT, Lanhydrock)
site facilities	

Boscastle

The natural inlet forming the harbour at Boscastle has proved an invaluable asset through the ages. With evidence of human activity here stretching back at least 4,000 years it is clear that we have had a significant impact upon the environment, and yet it remains one of the jewels in the crown of the Cornish coast, not only for its archaeological history but also for its natural history and beauty.

The name Boscastle is a shortened version of 'Boterelescastel', due to the building of a castle overlooking the valley by the de Botterell family in the twelfth century. It was then that many houses were first built in the village, but the harbour must have been in use long before that time. Examples of our historical influence can be seen on the promontory of Willapark, where there are remains of an Iron Age cliff castle; along the cliffs of California Quarry which, in the nineteenth century, were quarried for slate, and on Forrabury Common, where there is a field system dating back to the Dark Ages.

This field system, known as Forrabury Stitches, is being maintained using ancient techniques based upon a crop rotation cast aside by most farmers in Britain during the Middle Ages. It is one of only three examples managed in such a way across the whole of Britain. The four-year cycle allows the growing of crops such as barley and wheat for three years, followed by one year of pasture. Each year crops can be grown between Lady Day (25 March) and Michaelmas Day (29 September); outside of that period common grazing is practised over all 42 strips or stitches.

Recently conservationists have become aware that this field system supports a rare mixture of arable flowers now extinct across much of the agricultural

Boscastle harbour.

Left: Common fumitory is one of many arable weeds that can be found growing on Forrabury Stitches.
Right: The greater horseshoe bat has roosts in the area.

land in Britain because of the indiscriminate use of chemicals. Here we have corn marigolds, lesser snapdragon, fumitory, sun spurge and bugloss, among commoner but no less beautiful flowers, growing in a situation where they have been present for many hundreds of years. The field system is best viewed from Willapark, though there is a footpath through the fields to Forrabury Church.

Another habitat of interest is in the small but beautifully formed Valency Valley. This narrow valley has a mature oak coppice growing in the shelter offered by its steep sides. One of the key species of this site is the pearl-bordered fritillary which can be found here from late April to early June. The small pearl-bordered fritillary also occurs here.

It has long been known that Minster Church, in the Valency Valley, provides a safe roost for a colony of the rare greater horseshoe bat, but we haven't long understood the exact requirements of this endangered species. Conditions here are good for bats, in particular the mosaic of small fields surrounded by good-quality hedgerows and trees, which offers them a rich hunting ground, but they can be quite exacting in their requirements.

To the south of the valley an area of mixed farmland surrounds the tenanted Home Farm, owned by the National Trust. The management practices employed on the farm are geared to helping the bats where possible. Many of the meadows are farmed without the use of chemicals, in order to allow insects to flourish. It was only fairly recently realized that some chemicals used to worm cattle were having a negative effect on the greater horseshoe bats. We now understand that for a significant part of the summer these bats eat a lot of dung beetles, but where cattle are continually dosed with one particular type of worming agent their dung becomes sterile. Sterile dung is no good for dung beetles, and therefore no good for the bats. The solution is to use other agents for worming, or to use the chemicals more judiciously.

My own priority for a day trip to Boscastle is to walk the coast path to the south, taking in Forrabury Stitches *en route*. It is possible to walk as far as Tintagel and back, but it might be better to catch a bus one way. The coast path here is absolutely stunning, but it is one of those frustrating stretches of path where you think it isn't far to the next headland until you look at the route taken by the path!

The coast between Boscastle and Tintagel is at its best in spring, when flowers are everywhere. As beautiful as they are, I wouldn't suggest travelling a long way to Boscastle just for the flowers of the coast. What makes the coastline here extra special for the naturalist is seabirds, in particular auks. It is never easy to see auks in Cornwall – they tend to breed on islands and cliffs well out of our gaze, but here we have a chance to see, hear and even smell them.

These cauldrons and whirlpools are a feature of Rocky Valley between Boscastle and Tintagel.

Guillemots have a chocolate brown back.

The two species of auk that breed here are the guillemot and razorbill. They may be distinguished by bill shape if the view is good enough. Other features to help separate them include the following: the razorbill is black and white whereas the guillemot is dark brown and white; a razorbill looks plump compared with a guillemot; razorbills have a white line along the top of their bill; razorbills tend to breed on rocky scree and among rocks, while guillemots always nest on cliff ledges. If that isn't enough, then just enjoy the moment! It isn't possible to get anywhere near as close to these birds here as you will on the Scillies, but if seeing guillemots and razorbills makes the hair stand up on the back of your neck, then this will keep you going until you can get your next proper fix.

The top spots along here to find breeding seabirds are the islets just offshore, but they also breed on the cliff of the mainland. All of the islands between Boscastle and Tintagel have auks – the best are Short Island and The Sisters. My own experience suggests

Left: The razorbill has a distinctively shaped bill.
Right: Sea campion is common along the coast.

that Short Island is better for razorbills and The Sisters are better for guillemots; there are probably a few hundred pairs of each. As well as the auks there are shags, fulmars, herring gulls and great black-backed gulls on these small islands, while peregrine falcons and kestrels also nest nearby.

LOOK OUT FOR

Late April–early June: Pearl-bordered fritillary in Valency Valley.

Late May–early July: Small pearl-bordered fritillary in Valency Valley.

May–July: Flowers of the coastline include thrift, spring squill (May), wild thyme, kidney vetch, oxeye daisy and wild carrot. Breeding seabirds include shag, great black-backed gull, razorbill, guillemot and fulmar. In the Valency Valley dippers and grey wagtails raise their young along the river.

June–July: At Forrabury Stitches look for arable flowers. At sea possibly basking sharks.

All year: Interesting geology of the area. Look at cliff sections and the rock face at California Quarry, where you can see a cross-section through the geological history of the Carboniferous and Upper Devonian periods. Peregrine and kestrel are resident along the cliffs.

4

Walk on public rights of way

Explorer 106; *Landranger* 200

By road: From Wadebridge take B3314 N, follow signs to Polzeath

SW 936 789

To rock pools from Visitor Centre about 0.25 ml

2 hours for rock-pooling

Beach

Rock pools (nearby dunes and headland)

Rock-pooling area SW 933 797;
The Mouls SW 938 815;
Daymer Bay Dunes SW 929 775

AONB, SSSI (part)

Rock pool rambles led by North Cornwall Coast and Countryside Service

Rock pool rambles held in summer, otherwise open all year

Free

T: 01208 265 644 (NCDC Coast and Countryside Service)

Note: Dogs not allowed on beach in summer

Polzeath

Our marine environment is every bit as important as that which we cherish on land, but it hasn't always registered as highly in our consciousness. Our feeling of empathy with marine life may not be as strong as it is with the more familiar land-based wildlife, but we are beginning to realize that protecting the oceans is important, and that our actions have an impact on them.

Getting to grips with wildlife in the marine environment is not at all easy, since watching wildlife under water is at best difficult and in practice just not feasible for most of us. However, there is one way in which we can all begin to appreciate the world on the other side of the tide line, and that is through rock-pooling.

There are plenty of choices for a rock-pool ramble around the county, but I have picked Polzeath. Here there is a Voluntary Marine Conservation Area stretching from Daymer Bay to Pentire Point – a length of around three miles. This was established in July 1995, with the aim of encouraging people of all ages to become more involved in the marine environment. There is also a Marine Visitor Centre near the beach, which has information on what can be seen and how to see it safely, and a warden leads rambles around the rock pools during the summer in an area immediately to the north of Polzeath beach.

Going on an organized ramble has its advantages: you see anything caught by everyone in the group, and you benefit from the expert knowledge of the leader, which is of great value when entering a new area of wildlife-watching.

Let me whet your appetite with a few facts about wildlife in Cornish rock pools.

The view to Pentire Point from New Polzeath at high tide.

Did you know that female crabs can be distinguished from males by the size and shape of their tails? The 'tail' is found under their body, and is a triangular-shaped structure. In females the tail is much wider and is used for carrying eggs. Some female crabs lay as many as 180,000 eggs at a time. Did you know that crabs cast off their shell in order to grow? And if so, did you also know that at the same time they grow back any legs that they have lost? I didn't realize that male crabs hold on to females until they shed their skin, so that they can mate – hopefully they can sense when a shed is imminent, otherwise it could be a long wait!

In rock pools there are some herbivores and some carnivores. The limpet, for example, is a herbivore. When the tide is high it drags its tongue across the rocks, scraping off the algae as it slimes its way along, and when the tide begins to fall it follows its own mucus trail back to its 'home scar' – an indentation in the rock where it holds fast through each low tide.

The dog whelk, however, is a carnivore. Often a vibrantly coloured creature, its shell striped in various shades including black or orange, its eating habits are a little gruesome. It eats shellfish, such as mussels and limpets, by first drilling a hole through their shells, using a corrosive acid and a rasp-shaped tongue, before injecting an enzyme to digest the unfortunate creature inside its own shell – a process which takes about half a day. Once the mollusc has been made into a dog whelk's chowder it is sucked out and the whelk moves on to the next one. But the mussels are learning to fight back: if given the chance they can bind dog whelks to rocks, preventing them moving and often exposing them to the desiccating effects of the sun at low tide.

One of the most impressive fish that is likely to be encountered here is the sea scorpion. This fish has developed two defensive strategies. It can change colour to match its surroundings, giving it a wonderful, chameleon-like camouflage, and if that

Left: The Mouls and The Rumps.
Above: A trio of dog whelks.

doesn't work it can also change its size to confuse would-be predators. By puffing up its head the sea scorpion makes itself look too big for all but the largest assailants to tackle.

Did you know that one type of seaweed found here is commonly used as a thickening agent in foods and other products? Called Irish Moss, it is used in toothpaste, make-up, ice-cream and milk shake, as well as some beers and medicines.

Off the beach, but within walking distance of Polzeath, there are plenty of other interesting wildlife locations. To the north is the headland of Pentire, around which is a good circular walk. Traditional farming practices here make for a rich wildlife environment, but the one factor that makes this spot unique is that it is just about possible to see puffins from here. Puffins nest on the island known as The Mouls, and though this is a few hundred yards

Above: A male velvet swimming crab holds on to a female until she sheds her skin.
Right: The eggs of a Cornish sucker fish found under a rock.

offshore they can sometimes be seen fishing in the channel between the island and the mainland. I have never seen puffins from any other place on the mainland of Cornwall, so if you don't come here to see them then it will have to be the Isles of Scilly.

To the south of Polzeath is Daymer Bay, which, apart from a golf course, also has an area of dunes. These dunes are attractive for wild flowers such as knapweed, lady's bedstraw, wild thyme and pyramidal orchids, which attract almost equal numbers of butterflies, including the uncommon (in Cornwall) marbled white.

Left: The distinctive tentacles of the snakelocks anemone in a rock pool.
Above: A marbled white butterfly roosting on a knapweed flower at Daymer Bay.

LOOK OUT FOR

May–July: From Pentire Point look out for puffins; possibly basking sharks and sunfish.

Summer: On Daymer Bay dunes look for butterflies including marbled white, small copper, small heath, small and large skipper, and flowers such as lady's bedstraw, pyramidal orchid, knapweed and wild thyme.

In the rock pools: crabs (spider, shore, velvet swimming, edible, hermit); fish (common blenny, Montagu's blenny, goby, sea scorpion, wrasse, eel, pipe-fish, Cornish sucker); sea anemones (beadlet, strawberry, snakelocks); shellfish (mussels, limpets, barnacles, whelks); seaweed (ten species of special conservation importance); prawn, sea slater, starfish, Celtic sea slug, cuttlefish, sea squirts and sponges.

5

Walk on public right of way

Explorer 106; *Landranger* 200

By road: From Wadebridge take A39 S; turn R on A389 to Padstow. Park by harbour

SW 922 751

6 ml each way

3 hours if walking one way (cycle hire available in Padstow)

Easy walking or cycling conditions on a well-surfaced, disused railway line

Estuary, woodland, marsh

Pinkson Creek SW 947 734; Dennis Hill SW 922 741; Little Petherick Creek SW 923 737; Cant Hill SW 947 743

AONB, SAC

NCDC

All year

Free

T: 01208 265 642 (NCDC)

The Camel Estuary

Built in 1899, the railway line along the south side of the Camel Estuary linked the once busy harbour of Padstow with Wadebridge, and subsequently the mainline beyond Bodmin. The demise of this railway in 1967 was obviously a setback for people of the area, but the irony is that many more people now use this stretch of line than ever before – the difference being that they do so under their own steam.

Cornwall County Council established a cycleway here in 1984, and since then it has grown in popularity to the point where it now attracts several hundred thousand visitors each year, and millions of pounds for the local economy – and these numbers are growing annually. Of the many reasons for using the trail, one that is increasing is for watching wildlife, and there could be no easier route for getting into a rich environment, particularly for birds.

Padstow harbour regularly plays host to a group of friendly turnstones. These active waders can be seen on the harbour walls as well as on the stony shore nearby. Where there is more mud there will be dunlin, and where it is sandier there may be a small number of sanderling. In the channel of the River Camel, cormorants slip below the calm surface of the water in search of fish. Between fishing trips they perch on boats and posts, with their wings held aloft to dry.

The steep-sided Dennis Hill is a regular haunt of birds of prey. Buzzards, ravens and sparrowhawks use the thermals created on the side of the hill to gain height. Spring is a good time to watch them, when they are displaying to their partners by tumbling through the air and passing food to each other. If you visit in May, look out for early purple orchids alongside the main track here.

The Camel Estuary from Padstow.

Left: The dunlin is one of our smallest waders, at only 15 cm from tip to tail.
Above: Bullfinches are commonly seen along the trail.

Once across the railway bridge there is an alternative to continuing along the trail. From here it is possible to walk around Little Petherick Creek – another very interesting walk, particularly if you have walked the Camel Trail many times before.

The stretch of trail between Padstow and Pinkson Creek is always good for bullfinches. Their gentle 'few few' notes are constantly uttered to bring pairs closer together, but despite their persistence they can be difficult to locate. Once seen they will not be forgotten: the male has a stunningly rich, rose-red breast, and in flight both male and female reveal a clean white rump, a feature which is often the only physical clue to their identification.

There is a heronry at Pinkson Creek, and the herons can easily be watched as they feed in the channels

Little egrets are numerous all year round.

close to the trail. Standing is something that herons do well. They show little urgency, but this is their chosen hunting technique: waiting and watching; eventually a fish will break cover, disturbing the mud and shattering its one defence – camouflage. Immediately the heron strikes: boldly and without reservation it lunges its powerful neck and, more importantly, its dagger-sharp beak towards its prey. A successful strike leaves the fish impaled, and within seconds it will be turned and swallowed whole.

In stark contrast to the grey heron is the little egret, a bird found in good numbers along the Camel; the contrast is not only in colour and appearance, but also behaviour. If it is possible to appear graceful and gangly at the same time, then the little egret pulls it off. In flight the egret is one of the most relaxed and elegant of birds: with its neck folded and legs outstretched, its wings beat slowly to create this air of calm. But airs and graces are forgotten when the egret begins stalking, chasing fish around the shallows, flapping, swerving, darting and lunging.

Every turn of the track and every last cutting brings with it a slightly changed vista; the view towards Rock and beyond to the mouth of the estuary is striking. Opposite Pinkson Creek is Cant Hill, a dome-shaped hill caused by an igneous intrusion of dolerite hardening the bedrock, creating a mass of rock which has been more resistant to weathering

Otters are present on the River Camel, though they are never easy to see.

than its surroundings. It now stands proud of the rest of the landscape, making a readily identifiable feature. Badgers are much in evidence along the Camel Trail and, though you are unlikely to encounter one during daylight hours, it is often possible to see the dried grass that they use for bedding scattered across the trail adjacent to their pathways.

Towards Wadebridge the riverside changes from mud to marsh. Here in winter is a wide range of wildfowl, including occasional Bewick's and whooper swans, and some geese. On the water, goldeneye are regularly seen through the winter, together with rare grebes such as Slavonian and black-necked, as well as the commoner little and great-crested varieties. During autumn and winter in the creeks there are curlews, and both bar-tailed and black-tailed godwits.

The river around Wadebridge is perhaps one of the best places in Cornwall to see otters. There is no doubt that otters have forged a remarkable

Left: The curlew is present on the estuary for most of the year.
Right: The black-necked grebe is a rare winter visitor to the estuary.

comeback after a disastrous period in the 1960s and 1970s. They are now widespread across the county, but always very shy. To see them we need a mixture of field craft, patience, and good fortune. Otters are essentially nocturnal in Cornwall, but they become active at dusk so a summer's evening is probably the best time to try to see one. Calm conditions give us our best chance, because the otter is then more obvious as it breaks the surface of the water.

This route is used by a great many people, particularly during school holidays, so if you can avoid the busy times it would make sense to do so. Arrive early in the morning, out of the tourist season, and the Camel Estuary is hard to beat. Cycling is a good way to see this stretch of estuary, but to walk one way and catch a bus back is a good alternative.

LOOK OUT FOR

September–March: Wading birds include curlew, dunlin, redshank, greenshank, turnstone, sanderling, oystercatcher, black-tailed and bar-tailed godwits.

February–April: Activity among the grey herons at Pinkson Creek.

April–May: Whimbrel.

August–September: Regular sandwich terns and occasional ospreys on passage.

December–February: Probably the best season for birds, with waders at their most numerous. Also a variety of wildfowl, including regular wigeon, shelduck and goldeneye; occasional great-crested grebe, and red-breasted merganser; more rarely an odd white-fronted goose, Bewick swan, Slavonian and black-necked grebes.

All year: Little egrets are plentiful; otters may be seen here (try the Wadebridge end of the trail on a calm evening – one of the best rivers in Cornwall for this elusive mammal).

6

Walk on public rights of way

Explorer 104; *Landranger* 200

By road: From A3075 (Newquay to Truro) turn R shortly after leaving Newquay on minor road signed Crantock. Continue through Crantock to end of this road. Park in either of the pay and display car-parks

SW 776 606

39 ha/97 a

2 ml (approx)

2 hours

Hilly in places, but good footpaths

Arable fields, coastal grassland, beach, cliff

Porth Joke SW 772 606; Crantock Beach SW 780 610; Kelsey Head SW 765 608

NT

All year

Parking fee (private car-parks)

T: 01208 742 81 (NT, Lanhydrock)

Note: Light refreshments at pub

West Pentire

As a naturalist I appreciate the finer details or subtle, attractive colours of our natural world. The delicate purple of spring squill; the fascinating shapes and textures of an unrolling fern, or the enthusiastic, yet little-appreciated, song flight of a rock pipit are all examples that come to mind. Although these are all present at West Pentire, they are not what make this headland so breathtakingly spectacular. The beauty of this place is anything but subtle; it is unavoidable, unmistakable and unforgettable.

The National Trust has owned 39 hectares of the headland at West Pentire since 1960. Situated between The Gannel estuary and Porth Joke (also known as Polly Joke, a name derived from the Cornish *poll an chauk*, meaning 'the chough's cove'), it is in the centre of an exceptional area for wildlife. In particular, the fields of the headland are home to an extraordinary number of arable weeds.

The term 'arable weed' has come about through an historic dislike of flowers that grow among our crops. Throughout the history of cultivation we have tried to produce crops more and more efficiently by eliminating competition, without regard for our environment. Flowers have been removed, insects killed, and our land poisoned by chemicals. Fortunately, people are now taking an active interest in our natural heritage, and the National Trust is just one organization that is taking note.

In June and July it becomes difficult to get under the skin of this place, because the overall view, enhanced by fields of flowers, is so stunning. For just a few weeks each year, acre upon acre of arable fields is literally and liberally smothered in red and yellow flowers. In terms of colour and quantity, the fields are dominated by just two types – poppies and corn

Corn marigolds and poppies grow at West Pentire.

Above: Common poppies grow best when the fields have been ploughed in autumn.
Right: The bud of a common poppy (top). The rough poppy is one of three species of poppy found at West Pentire (bottom). Far right: Cowslips are common in spring.

marigolds – but in fact there are many more species to be found by the more observant naturalist.

The poppies at West Pentire are of three different types: common, rough, and long-headed. The common poppy is the species with which we are all familiar – its four, scarlet-red petals overlap lavishly. The long-headed poppy has a similar-shaped flower, though it is smaller and more orange. In the rough poppy, the four, dark-based petals are much smaller and do not overlap. The best way to tell them apart is to look at their seedpods: the long-headed poppy has a long seedpod, whereas the pod of the rough poppy is bristly.

Such is the association of arable weeds with our history that a great deal of folklore has grown up with them. The poppy is associated with headaches, blindness, and, specifically in Cornwall, with causing warts when handled. It is likely that we created this myth to discourage children from picking the flowers, and hence damaging the crops in which they grew.

The other common and obvious flower on this headland, the corn marigold, was introduced in Neolithic times. It was once known as the 'kissing plant', since its oil is said to soften the lips and create passion. Delve a little deeper among the arable weeds and you will find other specialist flowers of

Crantock and Newquay seen from West Pentire at dusk.

arable land – such delicate flowers as the field pansy, bugloss, lesser snapdragon, white campion, and both the small-flowered and night-flowering catchfly.

There is a battle at West Pentire, and this struggle is the complete antithesis of that on an arable farm. The land here is managed entirely for the benefit of arable weeds, but even with this assistance some of the grasses are starting to dominate. The irony is that whereas farmers have long used chemicals to defeat the arable flowers to improve productivity, here chemicals are used to defeat the grasses in an attempt to maintain the flowers!

Poppies thrive in soil that is disturbed, since they need the heat of the sun for their seeds to germinate, so here at West Pentire the fields are ploughed each year. For the germination of poppies it is best that fields are ploughed in the autumn, but in 2005 they were left unploughed in response to changes in the agricultural subsidy system. The Single Farm Payment scheme discourages autumn ploughing to minimize the threat of soil loss in fields left bare during winter. Had the fields been ploughed in early spring, the consequences might not have been so marked, but as it was the year 2006 was a disap-

The six-spot burnet moth is common on the headland.

On the rough grassland around the headland, watch out for the colourful six-spot burnet moth. This day-flying moth looks red and black from a distance, but on closer inspection can be seen to have a metallic sheen. In June and July, as well as seeing the moth, you may also see the glossy cocoons of its larvae on grass stems. Its caterpillar feeds on the leaves of bird's foot trefoil, which can also be seen in flower during the summer.

Specific directions aren't really necessary to get the best from this site: simply walk around the headland, and on the footpaths through the fields. A longer walk can be created by walking north to Crantock Beach, or south around Kelsey Head beyond Polly Joke.

pointing one for arable weeds on the headland. I am sure this was only a temporary blip, and that normal services will be resumed.

If you were to visit West Pentire just once, then it should be at the beginning of July, but that is not to say that it isn't worth visiting at other times of year. Other highlights include a splendid show of cowslips during April and May, particularly on the slopes down to Porth Joke. From May to July there is a wonderful selection of coastal flowers. Walking around the headland will bring you as close as you are likely to get on mainland Cornwall to a colony of nesting fulmars, but be careful if you go off the path, the cliffs here are dangerous.

LOOK OUT FOR

April–May: Cowslips are a tremendous sight; in damp sections, flowers of flag iris and ragged robin; spring squill on coast.

May–June: Typical coastal flowers include thrift, kidney vetch and sea campion. Buzzards nest in the valley above Porth Joke; whitethroats nest in most of the hedges. Kestrels hover over the longer grassland, searching for field voles. Look out for the fulmar colony near the tip of the headland.

June–July: The fields come to life with arable weeds, including three species of poppy: common, rough and long-headed; corn marigolds, white campion, field scabious, small-flowered catchfly, night-flowering catchfly, lesser snapdragon, corn parsley, sun spurge, black bindweed, charlock, wild clary, corn spurrey, shepherd's needle, bugloss and field pansy. Among the grasses, the false oat grass stands tall; skylarks are extremely common, and can be seen and heard in all the fields and around the headland. Butterflies are numerous, including wall and meadow brown; dingy, small and large skipper. The six-spot burnet moth is common around the coastal strip.

type of location	Walk on public rights of way and nature reserve
map	*Explorer* 104; *Landranger* 200
directions to start point	By road: Take A3075 S from Newquay; after approx 3 ml turn R, signed Cubert and Holywell. Park in main car-park in Holywell
starting point	SW 767 587
size	650 ha/1,600 a
length	7 ml (many shorter alternatives); details of guided walks on website
recommended time	4 hours
conditions	Rocky coast path and difficult walking on dunes sand
habitats	Coast, beach, dunes
points of interest	Holywell Bay SW 767 587; Ligger Point SW 757 581; St Piran's Church SW 767 564
landscape designation	SAC, SSSI
owner	Various. CCC manages the group responsible for the SAC
open	All year
entry	Free
enquiries	T: 01872 222 000 (Penhale Sands SAC Countryside Officer, CCC)
site facilities	*Note:* Light refreshments and lavatories at Holywell

Penhale Sands

Big isn't always beautiful, and size isn't everything, but at Penhale Sands we have a British record: reaching a height of 90 metres, these are the tallest dunes in the United Kingdom.

It is reckoned that this dune system began forming as long as 5,000 years ago. Despite their ever-changing, fluid nature they have been a focus of human activity through the ages, and so they are of special significance not only for their wildlife but also for the history that they try to conceal. Early field systems are still visible in the more stable sections of the dunes, and the spoils of mining can be seen, together with some adits and shafts. During the Second World War a mock airfield was established on part of the dunes to draw enemy planes away from the actual airfield at Trevellas near St Agnes. Along the coast, at Penhale Point, there is an Iron Age cliff castle and several Bronze Age barrows.

To many, the most significant historical remains relate to Saint Piran, Cornwall's patron saint. St Piran was said to have found his way to Cornwall from Ireland and set up his baptistery here. It is in his honour that many place-names were formed: Perranzabuloe, for example, is literally 'St Piran in the sand', and Perranporth is 'St Piran's Cove'. His oratory, built in the fifth or sixth century, is thought to be the earliest site of Christian worship in mainland Britain.

The oratory was buried by the shifting sands in around the tenth century, when an alternative church was built a short distance away, and it is now marked by a simple granite plinth. The newer church, adjacent to the stone cross visible to the east, now also lies in ruins. Each year people take part in the St Piran's Day March, walking across the dunes to the site of the oratory to join in a religious service.

Penhale Dunes from Ligger Point.

Above: Pyramidal orchids grow commonly on all of our dunes, along with lady's bedstraw (left). The fragrant orchid is also found on Penhale dunes (right).
Right: The view over Holywell Beach from Penhale Point.

The dunes are owned by a variety of different organizations. The main landowner is the Ministry of Defence (MOD), which owns 380 hectares; next is Bourne Leisure, which owns Perran Sands Holiday Park. Smaller parts of this Special Area of Conservation (SAC) are owned by Perranporth Golf Club, Perranzabuloe Parish Council, and local farmers.

The MOD area is probably the most interesting from the point of view of wildlife, since it has suffered the least disturbance. Unfortunately, this area is closed to public access, though there are occasional guided walks, which are highly recommended. However, a large area of the dunes is open to the public. My suggested walk is from Holywell Bay along the coast path to the south, around Ligger Point, along the edge of the beach, across the dunes then back to Holywell along road and path.

The whole area is good for cowslips in April and May; the sandy soil is very much to their liking. At around the same time the beach often plays host to migrating whimbrel. Around Ligger Point watch out for a pair of nesting kestrels, together with the usual ravens, and a few pairs of fulmars nesting on the cliffs.

On the dunes there are plenty of stonechats, and as many linnets as I can remember seeing anywhere in Cornwall. Skylarks are flourishing here, despite

Top: The underside of the wing of the silver-studded blue butterfly reveals its seven 'studs'.
Above: The upper wing of a male silver-studded blue is a vibrant blue.

their decline on arable farmland: it seems that marram grass is a more than suitable substitute for wheat or barley. Its tall stems provide cover in which skylarks can hide, while the gaps between its stands allow easy access for the skylark to drop down from the sky, and pathways in which it can move around. In June and July the dunes support a wide array of flowers, including pyramidal orchid, lady's bedstraw, eyebright and wild thyme. In the MOD area are a few flowers which are most uncommon across the rest of Cornwall: marsh helleborine is found here and nowhere else in the county, and fragrant orchid, musk mallow and spring gentian also grow here.

The flowers provide nectar for insects which include an impressive 11 'Red Data Book' species*. Twenty-seven species of butterfly and 107 species of moth have been recorded, and I wonder how many more are still to be found? Two butterflies which are special to the area are the dark green fritillary and the silver-studded blue butterfly.

Silver-studded blue butterflies are at home in two completely different habitats in Cornwall. They live on heathland, where their caterpillars feed on heather, and on dunes where they utilize bird's-foot trefoil. The appearance of the male and female butterflies couldn't be more different: males are a striking deep blue; females are a sooty brown. Silver-studded blues are incredibly small, with a wingspan of between ten and 18 millimetres (about ½ inch). Look closely at one of these butterflies with its wings closed, and you will see that the black spots on the outer edge of its under-wing have shiny blue spots within them – the 'silver studs' of the butterfly's name.

The dunes at Penhale Sands are unusual in that they have significant areas of freestanding water, particularly in winter and spring; they also support temporary rivers on beds of clay. The damp areas are home to dragonflies, grass snakes, water mint, and a colony of the rare shore dock. The short sward on the drier parts of the dunes provides perfect conditions

Marsh helleborine grows in damp sections of the MOD area.

for the growth of mosses and lichens, including the scarce, but amusingly named, scrambled egg lichen. Favouring the drier parts of the reserve is a species of spider, known rather formally by its scientific name *Gnaphosa occidentalis*, which is found at no other site in Britain, as far as we know.

*Note: The 'Data Books' were initiated by the International Union for the Conservation of Nature (IUCN), and list species that are threatened. To be listed in the 'Red Data Book', a species has usually shown a decline in its population or range of more than 50 per cent in the last 25 years. There are also 'Amber' and 'Green' Data Books which reflect less serious declines.

LOOK OUT FOR

March–September: Reptiles such as common lizards, adders and grass snakes.

April–May: Whimbrel on the beach; early flowering plants include cowslips, and both the early and spring gentians.

June–July: Pyramidal and fragrant orchids, wild thyme, mountain everlasting, stork's-bill, lady's bedstraw, carline thistle, water mint, shore dock, musk mallow, and the only Cornish site of marsh helleborine. Butterflies include the dark green and marsh fritillaries, and the tiny silver-studded blue.

Winter: Lichens and mosses grow well; there is a colony of the rare petalwort (a tiny liverwort which resembles a lettuce). Occasional short-eared owls on the dunes.

All year: Linnets, stonechats and skylarks are common.

8

Walk on public rights of way
and country park

Explorer 104; *Landranger* 203

By road: From A30 between
Redruth and Camborne turn off
at sign to Portreath and Tehidy.
At crossroads turn L then R
along South Drive, signed Tehidy
Country Park

SW 650 433

100 ha/250 a

4 ml

3 hours

Good quality footpaths

Mature woodland (deciduous and
coniferous), lakes, marsh, coastal
heath, cliff

Lakes SW 647 433;
Otter Bridge SW 646 433;
Deadman's Cove SW 627 434

AONB (coast), SAC (coast)

CCC

All year. No dogs around lakes

Free

T: 01872 222 000
(CCC Environment Service)

Note: Limited wheelchair access
around lakes; dogs not allowed
around lakes

Tehidy Country Park

In 1150 the Basset family bought the Tehidy Estate, and their family remained in residence until 1915. Their wealth derived from the many mines which they owned in the area, and the woodland of their new estate was to be coppiced to provide charcoal and timber for the industry. In the early eighteenth century, when it became fashionable among country gentry to create formal gardens on their estates, the Bassets followed suit by first planting trees to form windbreaks, and then using the shelter to grow more exotic species such as rhododendrons and laurels. Further landscaping was carried out in 1738, when the cascade was built from the pond; and in 1739 the pond, known as Parkan Pond, was developed into a lake to supply a source of fish and an attractive view from the mansion.

Since the family's departure the estate has changed hands frequently. At the beginning of the twentieth century it was bought by the County Council as a war memorial, but ownership then passed to the Cornwall Sanatorium Committee, who created a hospital to treat sufferers of tuberculosis. During this period part of the land was leased to the golf club, and the Forestry Commission took responsibility for management of the woodland, during which time a coniferous plantation was created. In 1983 the hospital closed, and the County Council acquired the estate once again to establish the Country Park that we have today.

The Country Park is now alive with ideas: local schools use it for activities; artists show their sculptures; youth groups use the camping area; a beautiful wildflower meadow has been created, and nature lovers are guided on walks by specialists to see fungi, badgers, flowers, and much more.

The cascade at Tehidy.

Mallards live on the lake.

There is obvious potential here for a great family day out. Children love the place because it is possible to feed ducks, swans, grey squirrels, and a wide range of garden birds by hand, but by making a circular walk to include the north coast, Tehidy can become a varied walk for the more serious wildlife enthusiast. I suggest parking at the main car-park accessed from South Drive. From here walk past the lakes,* and follow the river along its northern bank to the hamlet of Coombe. Take the footpath to the coast, and then go eastwards along the coast path before heading back into the Country Park from Bassett's Cove.

The lakes may be home to the commonplace, such as a flock of bread-grabbing mallards, mute swans, coots and moorhens, but there are often less common species too. A pair of little grebes nests here, and it is amazing how well hidden they remain. The lake is used by gulls for bathing; it is often visited by cormorants for fishing, and even a kingfisher some-times visits during the winter. Because the lakes are relatively small, close views are almost always guaranteed.

Indeed, you won't get closer to grey squirrels anywhere else in the county, and an interesting range of woodland birds also comes to feed from the

Grey squirrels entertain us with their antics.

hand. Blue tits, robins, great tits, coal tits, dunnocks, robins, chaffinches and greenfinches have all been tamed by many years of public support, while jays and nuthatches – usually very shy birds – come ridiculously close to pick up the odd peanut. Birds aren't the only wildlife around the water: dragonflies are numerous here, and bats can be seen hunting at dusk.

Leaving the lakes via the cascade, we soon come to Otter Bridge, so named because in the eighteenth century otters were trapped here for the gentry to hunt. They died out in the area at some point, but it seems that they have started to make a comeback, though

I have only ever seen mink on the lakes. The footpath from here passes through some attractive beech woodland, and then an area of coniferous trees.

The ground flora throughout the woodland is attractive in spring with bluebells, lesser celandines, wood anemones and wild garlic, and this is being enhanced by the removal of rhododendron and laurel to allow more light to penetrate to the ground during spring. This particular section of the walk is also impressive in autumn, when fungi grow among the leaf litter and rotting tree stumps. Possibly the most common fungus is the sulphur tuft, which grows in large numbers on rotting tree stumps. Its vibrant,

Left: Robins can be seen at the picnic table or going for a dip in the lake.
Above: Common birds such as the blue tit are very approachable at Tehidy.

sulphur-yellow colour also makes it one of the most obvious species. Look out too for the tall, scaly parasol mushrooms growing from the ground; and on mature trees you might see the artist's fungus, an unusual bracket fungus with a chalky white underside in which it is possible to write or draw with a stick (hence the name). One of the most beautiful mushrooms, growing mostly on beech logs, is called the porcelain fungus, which, as its name suggests, is almost pure white with a glossy, translucent quality. The most notorious toadstool is the fly agaric, whose classic red and white cap is extremely poisonous.

The path that cuts across to the coast passes along hedgerows through arable fields. In summer look out for whitethroats in the hedgerows, and skylarks in the fields; in winter there may be lapwings and golden plover. The coastal path on Reskajeage Downs offers a totally different set of possibilities. Here there are

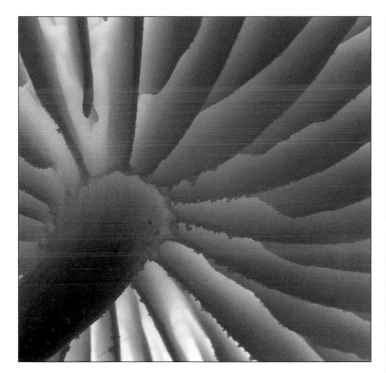

Left: The semi-translucent cap of a porcelain fungus. Right: The colourful fungus, fly agaric, can be found in autumn.

steep cliffs topped by a narrow strip of heath. Heather and both European and western gorse grow on top of the cliffs, and these are inhabited by the ubiquitous stonechats and linnets, while on the cliffs fulmars can usually be found. In the water around the base of the cliffs look out for grey seals, and further out to sea watch for passing seabirds, which can include gannets, kittiwakes and Manx shearwaters.

Finally, the return path leads through a mature area of deciduous woodland and past the new housing complex which was once the Bassets' home.

Note: Dogs are not allowed on the paths around the lakes, so quite a long detour around the house to the north will be necessary if you have a dog.

LOOK OUT FOR

February–April: Rooks nest above car-park at South Drive.

April–May: Flowers in the woodland include bluebell, primrose, lesser celandine, wood anemone, wild garlic and three-cornered leek. Little grebes are active on the main lake.

May–July: Ducklings and cygnets hatch. Badgers are quite numerous, but a late evening walk is essential to stand any chance of seeing them. Warblers in the woodland include blackcap, garden warbler and willow warbler. Flowers of the woods and lakes include meadowsweet, purple loosestrife and enchanter's nightshade. On the coast is wild carrot, yellow rattle, betony, knapweed and wood sage. Watch out for gannet, kittiwake, fulmar and Manx shearwater from the coast.

July–September: Heather, bell heather, western gorse on cliff tops.

September–October: Jays at their noisiest; fungi at their best.

Winter: Look for long-tailed tit, coal tit, goldcrest, nuthatch, great spotted woodpecker among the commoner species; many will feed very close, so take peanuts; kingfisher sometimes seen around the lakes; siskin may be seen.

All year: Skylark, linnet and raven on the coast.

9

Walk on public rights of way and nature reserves

Explorer 102; *Landranger* 203

By road: From Hayle take B3011 towards Portreath. After Gwithian turn L to Godrevy. Park at end of road

SW 582 430

6 ml from Godrevy to Upton Towans and back

4 hours

Sandy underfoot, but generally easy walking

Sand dunes, dune slack, headland, beach, cliff

Godrevy Head SW 581 433; St Gothian Sands Local Nature Reserve centred on SW 585 417; Upton Towans Wildlife Trust reserve centred on SW 578 400

AONB (part), LNR (parts), SAC (part), SSSI (parts)

NT (Godrevy), CWT (Upton Towans), CCC (St Gothian Sands)

All year

Car-park is NT, charge for non-members

Godrevy to Upton Towans

The section of coast from Godrevy Head along the towans towards Hayle is popular with tourists, dog walkers and surfers. It has been exploited by humans for centuries, in ways that have changed its face for ever, but today it is an extremely rich area for wildlife, with plenty of easy access and good walking.

The view of St Ives Bay from Godrevy Head is captivating, with the lighthouse making an obvious focal point for photographs – but don't forget that there is plenty of wildlife out there too. Nowhere in the county can we ever depend upon seeing dolphins, but St Ives Bay is certainly a favoured spot.

Two species of dolphin regularly occur in good numbers around Cornwall. The common dolphin tends to live further out to sea, and is most frequently seen in winter when 'super pods' have been recorded from special boat trips. It is common dolphins that are washed up dead on our shores because they get caught up in the nets of pair-trawlers fishing for bass. The dolphin that we are more likely to see from the coast is the bottlenose dolphin: we have a small, resident population of bottlenose dolphins in Cornwall, but they are very mobile and unpredictable.

From Godrevy, as well as the potential for seeing bottlenose dolphins, there are occasional sightings of harbour porpoises. It is easy to distinguish between the two species because of their behaviour. Porpoises only ever show a small amount of dorsal fin on a very dark, slightly hunched back, as they very briefly surface for air, whereas bottlenose dolphins are real show-offs, revelling in their ability

Gwithian Towans with Godrevy in the distance.

Bottlenose dolphins are very playful, often jumping out of the water.

to leap out of the water, often following boats in their search for attention.

The cliffs to the north-eastern side of the head are precipitous, but taking advantage of the safety they offer, a few pairs of shags nest on ledges. A little further around the head there is a good view down into Mutton Cove where, from autumn to spring at low tides, the little beach can be packed with grey seals. Grey seals come ashore to give birth, mostly in the autumn, so look out for the young, white-coated pups here.

Setting off to the south along the coast path brings us to an area which, for centuries, has been the subject of intense human interest. The Red River that cuts through between Godrevy Head and the Towans flows from the heart of mining country, and as such was historically the subject of intensive tin streaming. More recently, until 2005, sand was extracted at the rate of up to 25,000 tonnes per year, changing the face of the dunes dramatically. Commercial sand

extraction has now ceased, and this low-lying area of dunes has become a nature reserve named St Gothian Sands, owned by Cornwall County Council.

The final months of sand extraction were used to develop the site for wildlife, including the formation of a large lake complete with an island for breeding birds, and a couple of shallower areas of water, effectively dune slacks, for dragonflies and amphibians. A portion of this reserve will be out of bounds to the public, and will be maintained as a place for wildlife to exist undisturbed, but access along the coast is being improved, with the coast path being rerouted through the dunes instead of along the road. It will be very interesting to watch this reserve as it develops.

A little further south is the popular car-park at Gwithian. The pressure from beach-goers here is quite intense, but a few hundred metres further along the coast path it quietens down again. Beyond Gwithian we get into an area of dunes known as Upton Towans, which is owned by Cornwall Wildlife Trust. It is well

Porpoises show only a small dorsal fin as they swim by.

worth exploring inland of the coast path between here and the St Ives Bay Holiday Park.

The dunes of Upton Towans have not always been as quiet as they are today, for they were once the centre of a busy industry. At the beginning of the nineteenth century, the Cornish Kennall Vale Gunpowder Company began operations in Kennall Vale near Ponsanooth (where, coincidentally, the Wildlife Trust has another reserve – Site 25), and by 1887 they had sufficient demand to build a new site to produce dynamite. Upton Towans was the ideal location, since it offered an area clear of population but close to a labour force in Hayle and, importantly, the hilly topography of the dune system offered protection should any accidents occur. It seemed, at the time, that the Cornish tin-mining industry was in a period of expansion, so creating an increasing demand for their dynamite, and by 1890 the factory, then managed by National Explosives, was operational and producing 500 tonnes per year.

Demand was high, production increased, and 1,800 men were employed on site; a railway line was constructed to Hayle, as well as tramways across the dunes. The First World War drove demand even higher, and the government created new factories in other parts of the country to satisfy the needs of the armed forces. However, it became clear that as soon as the war ended there would be a massive over-production of explosives, and many companies would go to the wall. National Explosives had a good reputation for their quality of production, but their market contacts were not wide enough to compete with larger organizations. In 1917 they ceased production on this site, and the factory was stripped of its contents.

The features left behind by this industry now form important wildlife habitats. The mounds built around the buildings, to deflect accidental explosions upwards, provide shelter for insects and banks on which reptiles can bask. The old tracks used to

Grey seal pups can be seen in Mutton Cove, with most being born in the autumn.

transport materials around the site resist the growth of marram grass, allowing unusual lichens, mosses, liverworts (such as the rare petalwort) and succulents, such as the English and biting stonecrops, to take hold. Even the ruined remains of buildings are useful in providing microclimates of warmth for insects and reptiles to warm up.

There are still plenty of natural features in the dunes, including a couple of dune slacks, and these are at the centre of the best part of the dunes for wildlife. One of the gems of this reserve is the silver-studded blue butterfly, a tiny insect but with a most strikingly rich colour. Look too for the small pearl-bordered fritillary and dark green fritillary. There are plenty of orchids, primarily pyramidal, but also southern marsh. Scattered among the marram grass is the statuesque purple viper's bugloss, and among the shorter sward a vibrant mix of lady's bedstraw, storksbill, wild thyme and eyebright. There are a few bird species of note, including kestrel, linnet and stonechat, but the one that stands out from all the others is the skylark – there are few better places in Cornwall to enjoy the amazing song of this wonderful bird.

Above: The flowers of viper's bugloss can be seen on the towans during July.
Right: The dark green fritillary is on the wing in July.

WARNING: There are a lot of reptiles here, including adders. Adders are beautiful, with amazing camouflage. They are our only poisonous snake, and must be treated with respect. It is not uncommon for dogs to be bitten by them on the Towans, so some people avoid walking dogs here in spring and summer.

WHEELCHAIRS: Limited parking at SW 580 396. The gate is either unlocked or has a RADAR lock. The old tramways, although a little bumpy, provide access into the heart of Upton Towans Nature Reserve.

LOOK OUT FOR

May–June: Small pearl-bordered fritillary; skylarks breeding and singing.

June–July: Silver-studded blue butterfly, dark green fritillary, southern marsh and pyramidal orchid. In the late evenings look for glow-worms.

May–July: Yellow bartsia, viper's bugloss, sea spurge, variegated horsetail, twiggy mullein, common centaury, western clover, musk thistle, cowslip, ray's knotgrass, sea buckthorn, balm-leaved figwort and dune fescue. A sizeable colony of a rare mining bee burrows into the gravel near the mouth of the Red River.

July–August: Sea holly in great quantity at the south end of St Gothian Sands. Sandpipers around the pool.

August–September: Autumn lady's tresses, and some wax gill fungi (*Hygrocybe* sp.) grow in the dunes.

September–December: Best time to watch grey seals: pups being born.

Autumn–Winter: Snow buntings occasionally seen around the head. After storms check the tide-line for goose barnacles and by-the-wind-sailors.

Winter: Best time to see petalwort – a tiny, rare bryophyte resembling a lettuce, which grows on the old surfaced paths. On the beach look for waders including oystercatcher, ringed plover and sanderling.

All year: the headland is good for rock pooling; kestrels nest in the area and regularly hunt over the dunes; bottlenose dolphins and harbour porpoise possible.

10

The Hayle Estuary

Walk on public rights of way
and nature reserve

Explorer 102; *Landranger* 203

By road, Hayle: Turn off A30 at roundabout for St Ives, follow signs to Hayle
– this is The Causeway. After about
0.5 ml turn R on to minor road signed
St Erth; before railway turn R into
RSPB car-park. Copperhouse: From
Hayle Estuary along The Causeway
to Hayle, L at roundabout nr viaduct.
Road follows estuary, then bends R;
take small turn L over narrow bridge;
turn R. Park on R by swimming pool

For Hayle Estuary and Carnsew
Pool: SW 550 363. For Copperhouse
Creek: SW 558 377

151 ha/377 a

Half a day

Road, track, muddy path

Estuary, scrub, salt-water pool

RSPB car-park SW 550 362; hide
SW 548 362; viewing points estuary
SW 547 364, SW 544 364; Carnsew
Pool SW 554 373; Black Bridge
SW 567 382; Copperhouse car-park
SW 558 377; orchids SW 543 362

SSSI

RSPB

All year

Free

T: 01736 711 682 (Marazion Marsh)

Compared with our other estuaries, including the Tamar, Fal and Camel, the Hayle Estuary is very compact and easy to watch. The Hayle Estuary also benefits from being the most westerly of them all, so more frequently attracts rare waders and greater interest among bird-watchers.

The RSPB owns most of the estuary, both at Hayle and Copperhouse, having purchased it for the princely sum of £1 in 1991. Ryan's Field was purchased later, in 1995, and has been allowed to revert to a salt marsh in order to provide wading birds with a place to roost on high spring tides. The estuary has unusually high levels of heavy metals left over from the mining era, but where the surface is left untouched a healthy layer of mud forms a barrier, locking away the toxic mud underneath, so birds can find food here. The most highly contaminated area is that of Ryan's Field; there is little food for wading birds here, and that is why they only use this field when forced off the estuary.

The main part of the estuary, between The Causeway and Lelant Saltings railway station, is certainly the most frequently watched and it is not uncommon to see a line of twitchers with telescopes set up along The Causeway when there is a special bird in residence. There are two important considerations when planning a visit: one is the time of year; the other is the state of the tide. Interest tends to peak in September, when there is the best chance of an unusual wader, and then again in the winter, when the number of birds is at its greatest with waders and wildfowl, as well as the possibility of some rarer wildfowl and gulls. Ideally, a visit should start a couple of hours before high tide, so that as the tide rises birds

The Old Quay House Inn from
The Causeway in winter.

The hide at Ryan's Field.

are pushed closer to The Causeway. When the tide is fully in it might be worth having a look from the road that passes the Old Quay House Inn. Just beyond the inn is a point which gives a good view of the high-tide roost, though if the tide is very high birds can be driven off the estuary completely. It is then that Ryan's Field is at its best.

Ryan's Field can be watched from the hide near the RSPB car-park, or from The Causeway. There is a footpath from the hide to the road, and a circular route including a length of the road is possible from here. The scrubby vegetation around the pools near the hide is good for breeding birds such as reed warbler, sedge warbler and reed bunting, but there is most interest here in autumn and winter with waders and wildfowl.

A little further along The Causeway towards Hayle we come to Carnsew Pool, which has a footpath around its entire edge, and this is an excellent walk at any state of tide, but is probably best at low tide. The footpath leads into the main part of the estuary, as well as giving good views of the pool. When the tide is out the pool has a wonderful muddy margin, and because the sides of the path are often well vegetated

Above: Great northern divers are regulars at Carnsew Pool.
Right: Lapwings often roost on the marsh at Copperhouse Creek.

it is sometimes possible to approach waders closer than might otherwise be the case. The birds that can be seen from here are the same as those on the main estuary, but with the added interest provided by divers and grebes in winter.

For me the most special bird occurring here each winter is the great northern diver. I don't know of anywhere else that can offer such consistently good views of this species. To optimize your chances of seeing one, visit the pool after a period of stormy weather in January or February. As well as the great northern diver it is sometimes possible to see black-throated diver here and, rarely, a red-throated diver. Divers in winter plumage can be difficult to tell apart, but the great northern diver is much bulkier than the others, and has a very angular-shaped forehead which is diagnostic. At this time of year there should also be great crested grebes and little grebes; occasionally there may be a Slavonian or black-necked grebe.

Above: In winter the Hayle Estuary is alive with ducks – mostly wigeon.
Left: The curlew sandpiper is one of the regular rare birds here (this one is in moult).

Where the water flows out of the pool into the estuary, watch out for kingfishers, particularly in winter.

The remaining part of the estuary is at Copperhouse Creek, which has a road along its northern edge, making it an easy place to watch. Its creek is never so deep as to mask any of the birds' presence, so it is probably best to visit this location at low tide, though it can be interesting to watch as the tide rises. As well as the muddy creek there is an area of marsh around the Black Bridge at the top of this estuary, which looks worthless but can be good for birds, particularly if a high tide occurs in the early morning (before dog walkers disturb everything!). The species of bird seen from here are slightly different from those of the main Hayle estuary, although they overlap greatly. Specifically, I would suggest looking out for kingfishers in winter from the Black Bridge,

Bee orchids can be found growing on the A30 roundabout.

variety of orchids. The most common is the southern marsh orchid, followed by the pyramidal orchid but, most surprisingly, there is also a good population of bee orchids. It is thought that these orchids were accidentally brought in with the topsoil when the roundabout was created. The best place to look for bee orchids is in the triangle leading from the round-about towards Lelant, and the best time is mid-June, but only if the grass hasn't been cut!

and often there is a very large flock of lapwing and golden plover here among the Spartina grass in very cold winter weather.

Ending on a slightly quirky note, there is a very unusual spot for some rare and attractive species of flower near the Hayle Estuary. Where The Causeway meets the A30 there is a large roundabout, and on the verges here there are a surprising number and

---

LOOK OUT FOR

April–May: Whimbrel.

June: Orchids, including pyramidal (late June), southern marsh and bee (mid-June); common broomrape along The Causeway.

August–September: Occasional osprey on passage, common sandpiper.

September–October: Good for curlew sandpiper and little stint on the main estuary, as well as other, rarer waders.

September–March: Waders include curlew, dunlin, black-tailed and bar-tailed godwits, oystercatcher, redshank, greenshank, ringed plover, grey plover, little egret and grey heron; kingfishers could be seen any-where.

December–March: At Carnsew Pool look for great northern diver, little grebe and great crested grebe; sometimes other rarer grebes and divers. On the main estuary look for wigeon, shelduck and teal; occasional American wigeon, green-winged teal and other rare wildfowl. Gulls often include Mediterranean and ring-billed. At Copperhouse perhaps a flock of golden plover and lapwing. Also look for snipe here; occasional Bewick's or whooper swans. Peregrine, kestrel and sparrowhawk often seen hunting.

All year: Plants on the salt marsh include glasswort, perennial glasswort, sea arrow grass, sea purslane, common reed and soft rush.

type of location	**Town**
map	*Explorer* 102; *Landranger* 203
directions to start point	**By road: Follow signs to St Ives from A30 W of Hayle, or park at Lelant Saltings Park and Ride; also signed from A30**
starting point	**SW 518 407**
length	**In town: 2 ml; if walking from Lelant Saltings: 5 ml**
recommended time	**3 hours**
conditions	**Easy walking on road and pavement; care needed on pier where ropes cross path close to edge**
habitats	**Coastal, town, headland**
points of interest	**Smeaton's Pier SW 521 408; The Island SW 520 412; Park and Ride, Lelant Saltings SW 543 365**
open	**All year**
site facilities	

St Ives

It may seem strange to devote a chapter of this book to the bustling harbour town of St Ives. It certainly doesn't fit into the same mould as a nature reserve, but because of its large number of human visitors St Ives offers the naturalist some unique opportunities. Another advantage to St Ives is that it will appeal to a broad spectrum of people – a distinct benefit to the keen naturalist with the demands of a family.

Where animals are subjected to people for long periods they become accustomed to our presence, and allow a much closer approach. In St Ives, and many other harbour towns, there are some species of bird and mammal that allow ridiculously close inspection. If you are interested in photographing wildlife, then this is a great place to start.

The most obvious residents of the town, in an ornithological sense, are the gulls. 'Seagulls' have a very bad reputation in St Ives, but it is only the herring gulls that have learned to take chips and ice-creams from passers by. I find it difficult to dislike them for evolving to the training we have given them, but I think we can all agree that it would be better for all if we were able to retrain them not to take food from us – so feeding the gulls is definitely off the menu.

Even without deliberate feeding there are plenty of opportunities for the gulls. On Smeaton's Pier fishermen discard bits of their catch – the odd, unwanted shellfish, for example. Herring gulls nip down, pick up the mollusc, and fly up into the sky before dropping it on to the pier to break the shell. If they are quick enough they fly down and consume the contents; if they aren't, then another gull gets in first. I have seen gulls in St Ives dropping starfish in a similar way: they can't swallow a whole one, but eventually an arm will break off and they will swallow that!

St Ives harbour from Smeaton's Pier.

Above: The great black-backed gull can be seen in St Ives.
Left: The herring gull in winter plumage has a brown spotted head.

Most people visiting St Ives will not care that other types of gull frequent the harbour, which is a shame since some, such as the great black-backed gull, allow excellent views here. The slate-grey back and larger size of the great black-backed gull distinguish it from a herring gull, and its pink legs are enough to separate it from the lesser black-backed gull, which has yellow legs. Any of the gulls found in Britain could be seen in St Ives, particularly in winter, but throughout the year it is possible to compare the plumages of gulls at different stages of their lives,

Above: The starling is a real character, and has a great voice.
Left: Perched on the wall of Smeaton's Pier this turn-stone was very relaxed!

gradually changing from the brown of a first-year bird to the grey and white of an adult.

Gulls are not the only scavengers in town. House sparrows and starlings both occur here in good numbers, and though we may consider them common that doesn't mean they aren't colourful characters. I particularly enjoy the starlings in late winter and early spring, when they are establishing territories. At the same time as their plumage develops its most wonderful metallic sheen, the starlings take to the railings, lamp posts, balconies and roofs to sing their hearts out. Although their song may not be as melodic as a warbler's, it is one of the most expressive of our

Above: Grey seals frequent the harbour at high tide.
Left: Rock pipits can usually be found on Smeaton's Pier at the harbour.

common birds. Later in the year, during autumn and winter, each day, just before darkness falls, starlings congregate in large numbers around St Ives. Many fly to Marazion Marsh (Site 19) for a safe roost, but some years a large flock stays in town, creating a fantastic sight as they wheel in unison above the houses.

From August through to May there are turnstones around the harbour. Their numbers reach a peak in winter, but their plumage is best in spring. They trot along the edge of Smeaton's Pier without a care in the world. Of course, turnstones should be turning stones or pushing and pulling at seaweed in the hope of finding small crustacea, but these birds find it easier to pick up scraps from the pier.

The lesser black-backed gull has yellow legs.

From Smeaton's Pier I have also had wonderful views of the normally shy rock pipit, as well as both shag and cormorant. Once I was privileged enough to see a shag hopping up the steps on to the harbour wall, where it was duly hand fed (with small fish) by a child not much taller than the bird itself. After digesting for a while it hopped back down the steps and into the sea.

If it is high tide then you will probably see grey seals from the pier – they have taken to following the fishing boats into the harbour, hoping for a tasty morsel. This habit, like feeding the gulls, could lead to aggressive behaviour in seals, and should be discouraged. Don't forget to look out to sea from the harbour wall, because St Ives Bay is a good location for seeing the local pod of bottlenose dolphins, but they are mobile so this is a long shot. Increase your chances by watching the birds: if you see a group of gannets diving then there is obviously a shoal of fish nearby, and that is the place to look for dolphins.

If there is a lot of activity among the seabirds then it is worth a walk to The Island, particularly if you visit between August and October. The bay of St Ives is a perfect 'trap' for migrating seabirds. Birds intending to stay further from land can be blown by strong westerly winds into the sea to the north of St Ives, and if the wind subsequently veers to a northerly then these birds will be encouraged into St Ives Bay on their way back out to the ocean. Since St Ives Island is a promontory (not in fact an island), this is the closest we can get to them. You will need binoculars to get good views; many keen birders use a telescope here for extra magnification.

Any Cornish harbour town plays host to some of the species mentioned here, but St Ives seems to offer the best wildlife opportunities of them all. To explore the town, either park in the town at one of the many car-parks or, in summer, try the park and ride from Lelant Saltings railway station, which also overlooks the Hayle Estuary (Site 10). If you fancy a good walk, it is possible to walk from Lelant Saltings along the coast to St Ives, and then get the train back. This route leads across Porth Kidney Sands, which are also good for wildlife.

LOOK OUT FOR

February–April: Starlings singing, listen for their mimicry; spring migrants such as wheatears on The Island.

August–October: Best time for sea-watching from The Island. Potentially, roughly in decreasing order of probability, you could see: gannet, fulmar, Manx shearwater, razorbill, guillemot, puffin, any of the British terns, great skua and Arctic skua. Less likely but possible species include: great shearwater, Cory's shearwater, Mediterranean shearwater, storm petrel, pomarine skua, long-tailed skua, Leach's petrel, Wilson's petrel, grey phalarope and Sabine's gull.

October–February: Look out for roosting flocks of starlings.

Winter: Seabirds may shelter in the bay, look out for great northern divers.

All year: Rock pipit, turnstone (probably not around in June and July), gulls, cormorant, shag and gannet; grey seals are regulars in the harbour at high tides, and bottlenose dolphins may be seen out to sea.

Walk on public rights of way

Explorer 102; *Landranger* 203

On B3306 from Pendeen to Zennor, park in lay-by adjacent to Carn Galver engine house

SW 422 365

7 ml

4 hours

Typical coast path, some rocky and wet stretches

Heath, farmland, cliff, marsh, scrub

Bosigran Cliff Castle SW 417 370; Porthmeor Cove SW 424 375; Gurnard's Head SW 432 387

AONB, RIGS, SSSI

Mostly NT

All year

Free

T: 01208 742 81 (NT, Lanhydrock)

Gurnard's Head public house in Treen

Note: Refreshments in pub at Treen

Bosigran and Gurnard's Head

The stretch of coastline from Bosigran to Gurnard's Head offers fantastic scenery – probably the best on the north coast of the Penwith peninsula. There are plenty of opportunities to excite the natural history enthusiast, while evidence of our occupation here between two and three thousand years ago adds to the interest.

Probably the most exciting early man-made features in this area come in the form of defensive fortifications at Bosigran Castle and Gurnard's Head, both of which were constructed in the late Iron Age. These headland castles occupy commanding positions, and used the natural defence offered by the steep sea cliffs on three sides. Both had walls, built to provide defence from the landward side, which can still be seen today. The castle on Gurnard's Head is even more interesting because it also has a selection of hut circles behind the defensive wall, situated in two groups. The example at Bosigran has no evidence of habitation, suggesting that it may have been used only for certain purposes, such as for trading.

Through most of history people have made only light use of this challenging environment, and little has changed. More recently, since the 1960s, the land between Bosigran and Porthmeor Valley has been owned by the National Trust, and rare breeds of sheep and cattle have been introduced to the coastal strip, where they have helped to bring the bracken under control. Being very old breeds, the Manx Loghtan sheep and Galloway cattle somehow look at home in this ancient landscape, and the effects

Gurnard's Head seen from Porthmeor Point.

of their controlled grazing can now be seen in the prominence of spring flowers.

The starting point for this suggested walk is at Rosemergy, a very good spot for cuckoos in May and June: listen for the familiar call of the male, and if you are fortunate you may hear the female replying with her soft, bubbling notes. They often call in flight and, since there are few perches in this area, it should be possible to locate one. From here walk down through the small copse, where you might see or hear migrant warblers in spring or autumn. The most likely are whitethroat, willow warbler and chiffchaff, but there could be others, including grasshopper warbler.

Once you reach the coast path at Porthmoina Cove the vegetation becomes much shorter – the effect of wind and sea spray stunting its growth – which allows some less common flowers to compete. You will notice the small, pink flowers of lousewort, a semi-parasitic plant that takes some water and nutrients from the roots of a host plant. Sensing the slight increase in temperature, the heath spotted orchids pluck up the courage to raise their heads in May. The delicately coloured, pink and white flowers contrast with their dark green spotted foliage.

Half a mile to the west of here a colony of kittiwakes nests at the base of the cliffs. You may be able to see them flying around at sea.

Take some time on Bosigran Head to look at the granite wall which is the basis of the original fortification built some 2,000–3,000 years ago. The banks around this wall are excellent for spring flowers, such as thrift and sea campion. The Manx Loghtan sheep are used to graze the rugged stretch of boulder-strewn terrain between here and Porthmeor Cove.

Left: Inland of the coast path at Gurnard's Head is the most spectacular field of thrift.
Top right: Lousewort grows around Bosigran.
Right: Spring squill has benefited from the coastal grazing around Bosigran.

Gannets can often be seen fishing in the bay near Gurnard's Head.

Walking east along the coast you will soon come to an outstanding view of this attractive cove. The quartz veins in the rocks on the far side of the cove were caused by the igneous intrusion of granite into the surrounding greenstone bedrock. Much of this area has been classified as a Regionally Important Geological Site (RIGS).

This length of path crosses some quite wet ground and, due to the recent grazing regime, large swathes of the nationally rare royal fern grow here. Look out for linnets using the water for bathing and drinking:

the males have stunning red breasts and ginger backs, but in flight they reveal a mixture of black and white wing markings. In the valley bottom, where there is more shelter, you are likely to encounter a pair of stonechats. Stonechats are among our most obvious birds, and are frequently encountered around the coast of Cornwall. They perch on top of gorse bushes, fence posts, or anything else that stands clear of surrounding vegetation, and they are rarely quiet. Their excited pebble-tapping call is the reason for their name.

Stonechats are distinctive birds of the Cornish coast.

Continuing along the coast, you will soon have Gurnard's Head in sight. The flowers along this section of path are typical of any coastal path in Cornwall, but the quantity takes some beating. Spring squill, which starts flowering in April, is still seen in May, whereas thrift, kidney vetch, sea campion and oxeye daisies reach their crescendo in May and June. Along the small hedge adjacent to the path, and in the field inland of this, the flowers of thrift form a patchwork of varying shades of pink. The sunlight and breeze play with the blooms, creating a ceaseless display of light, colour and movement.

On the path down to Gurnard's Head there is a proliferation of wild carrot growing through the longer grass, its white, spherical heads most numerous in June. There may be occasional butterflies taking advantage of the abundant nectar – one of the most common here is the wall brown. This is also an excellent location for the unusual oil beetle: an insect with a rather complex life cycle, its bulbous body and blue-black colour make it quite easy to identify.

Gurnard's Head is a great place for a picnic with entertainment. Gannets fly over from their nearest colony on Grassholm, an island off the coast of south-west Wales, specially to dive for fish in these waters. Shags nest along the coast, and can be seen diving for fish – they tend to jump up to gain the momentum to submerge, but once under water they have the ability to stay under for a couple of minutes, and can swim in pursuit of prey. If you prefer to eat indoors, then the Gurnard's Head pub is not far away in Treen. To create a circular walk, it is possible to walk back a short distance along the road and then along the inland footpath through Bosigran Farm. Enjoy walking through hay fields with meadow flowers, on land where chemicals are obvious by their absence, and look out for the pedigree Belted Galloway cattle – they are friendlier than they look!

LOOK OUT FOR

February–March: The wheatear is the first migrant to return.

April–May: Flowers of the coast include spring squill, thrift, kidney vetch, sea campion and lousewort.

May–June: Whitethroat and cuckoo at their most obvious; chiffchaff and willow warbler settle down to breed. Flowers include oxeye daisy, heath spotted orchid, and wild carrot. Look for oil beetles on grassy areas; emperor moths lay their eggs on the heath.

May–July: Kittiwakes can be heard nesting on the cliffs; royal fern grows in the damp patches near Porthmeor; six-spot burnet moths are on the wing. A late evening visit to nearby Carn Galver could be rewarded by the churring of a nightjar.

July–September: Manx shearwater often seen offshore in the evenings. Look for caterpillars of emperor moths on the heath areas.

September–October: Migratory birds including warblers in the scrub; shearwaters, skuas, terns at sea; hirundines (swallows and martins) along the coast.

All year: Peregrine falcon, raven, kestrel, gannet, grey seal, stonechat, linnet and shag.

type of location	**Walk on public rights of way**
map	*Explorer* 102; *Landranger* 203
directions to start point	**By road: In St Just take minor road towards Cape Cornwall; turn L immediately before school, signed (small sign!) to Cot Valley (road has speed bumps and is very narrow); follow it to very end – above cove called Porth Nanven**
starting point	**SW 357 308**
length	**Open**
recommended time	**3 hours**
conditions	**Roads, tracks, and rocky paths**
habitats	**Scrub, coast, pebble beach, mining waste**
points of interest	**Porth Nanven cliff and beach SW 355 309**
ape designation	**AONB**
owner	**NT**
enquiries	**T: 01208 742 81 (NT, Lanhydrock)**
nearest facilities	**St Just**
site facilities	

Cot Valley

Cot Valley, near St Just (in Penwith), just can't keep itself out of the spotlight – whether it is conservationists, gardeners, photographers or twitchers, there always seems to be something of interest or debate in this small valley. On the face of it, the valley seems like a fairly insignificant place, but then why should it receive adulation from such a diverse range of people? The answer lies in an equally diverse range of aspects, which include geographical position, geology, archaeology, and an invasive weed.

The valley's geological formation is critical. At the mouth of the valley lies Porth Nanven, a picturesque little cove with a most unusual cliff behind it. The lower half of the cliff consists of smoothly rounded granite boulders packed into a sediment of sand and grit. We can be sure that these boulders were worn by the abrasive action of the sea; over many thousands of years they were rolled around, gradually smoothing their surfaces against each other. Then, about 100,000 years ago, a long period of severe cold caused a greater quantity of ocean at the poles to freeze, and with more water being locked away as ice, both on land and at sea, the levels of the oceans dropped. The boulders that had been in the sea were now heaped up on a raised beach, and sediment gradually gathered to fill in the gaps.

Later still the effects of freezing on the valley sides caused shards of rock to slip down to the bottom of the valley. This periglacial flow resulted in the deposits that we now see in the upper section of the cliff. Over the last 10,000 years the levels of the oceans have gradually risen again, and the brutal force of its waves has cut into the sediment to reveal a cross-section of recent geological history. Some of the beautifully rounded boulders have been freed

The view from Porth Nanven towards Sennen.

Left: The cliff at Porth Nanven reveals a cross-section through time.
Above: Rounded boulders and limpets on the beach.

from their incarceration, and are once more at liberty to roll around on the beach.

These boulders have become an attraction for many visitors to the valley. The photographers, who love their shape and use them as a foreground to

In late summer the combination of bell heather and western gorse creates a blaze of colour.

their images, have done no harm, but others, who also admired them, were tempted sufficiently to take them away. Some, realizing the error of their ways, actually returned the stones under cover of darkness. It is now an offence to take any of the stones, and rightly so – we should all have the opportunity of seeing them where they belong.

It is obvious that the whole area was very heavily mined; the lodes of tin contained within the granite were the reason for much of this human activity. Although there are no large engine houses still standing here, there are a number of mills, leats, adits, shafts and spoil heaps. One of the most spectacular features is in the cliff face just to the south of Porth Nanven, at the base of Hermon Hill. Here a vertical lode was mined at different levels, forming an unusual complex of entranceways which can still be seen today.

In the ruins adjacent to the parking area at the end of the valley is a concrete buddle – a circular settling pool used for separating the tin from other sediments. This buddle now floods naturally, creating a haven for toads and palmate newts, among other pond life. At the top of the section of valley owned by the National Trust is a mill, where it is still possible to see the wheel pit and leat system. The heaps of spoil left over from the mining era, which litter the sides of the valley, may seem like eyesores, but they

Left: Common lizards bask on the mining spoil.
Right: Rare birds such as the hoopoe can be seen in
Cot Valley during times of migration.

are actually protected sites and offer excellent habitat to basking reptiles, including common lizards, and a variety of insects. The old shafts that have been collared with granite walls, for our safety, are home to several bat species.

When considering the shape and position of Cornwall on a global scale, it is easy to see that Cape Cornwall is in a unique position, jutting out into the Atlantic between Ireland and France. Migrant birds from east and west find themselves here in spring and, more particularly, autumn, to the delight of bird-watchers and twitchers from around the country.

Birds usually migrate at night and those that, come daybreak, accidentally find themselves on the cliffs of Cornwall make their way into the sheltered valleys. After resting and feeding, they will try to get their bearings and, if the weather is favourable, head off to the south during the following night. Unusual species with even more unusual names, such as red-

eyed vireo, wryneck and gyr falcon, have been seen here. This cosmopolitan blend of species represents America, Scandinavia, and possibly Iceland, but add to this a yellow-browed warbler from Asia and a hoopoe from the Mediterranean, and a suggestion of chaotic delight is formed in the mind.

I remember clearly my first visit to Cot Valley in the early 1990s. My experience was generally positive, but I was struck by the overwhelming growth of the pernicious Japanese Knotweed alongside the river. The first knotweed to grow here may have been dumped with garden waste, or it may have escaped from a garden further upstream – either way it had spread like wildfire, and was smothering all of the natural vegetation on the river's banks. The National Trust, reluctant to use chemicals, tried cutting it back regularly, but to little effect. In 2001 a radically new approach, trialled in North Cornwall, was used here. Labour-intensive in the extreme, this new approach was about to take ten people eight weeks to complete.

The yellow scales lichen grows on rocks above the high-tide line.

and those were significantly weakened. By 2003 only two people were needed for two days to inject the remaining stems, and the natural vegetation was recovering. This is a remarkable success story, which amazed and thrilled everyone. The treatment employed here is now used as an exemplar for others facing similar problems.

This beautiful valley, which lies at the very edge of our county, is likely to remain at the centre of our attention – let's hope for all the right reasons.

The work involved cutting each stem to about 30 centimetres from the ground, inserting a spike to break the sections inside each stem, and injecting Glyphosate into every one! The poison was absorbed by the rhizomes of the plant and did not affect the surrounding vegetation. In 2002 there was some re-emergence of knotweed, but probably only about 20 per cent of the previous year's plants had survived,

---

LOOK OUT FOR

February: Common toads spawn in the buddles.

April–May: Woodland flowers such as bluebells in the valley; coastal flowers such as thrift and sea campion.

Summer: Adders, common lizards and slow worms use the mining spoil heaps to bask – look for them in the mornings. Birds breeding include whitethroat, chiffchaff and blackcap. Rock samphire grows on the headland; wild carrot is common.

September–October: The season for migratory birds as well as the common British migrants, such as redstart and pied flycatcher. There are regularly scarce migrants such as red-breasted flycatcher, firecrest, barred warbler, black redstart and wryneck. Rare migrants such as Arctic warbler, Pallas's warbler and sub-Alpine warbler, and mega-rarities such as Swainson's thrush also occur here occasionally.

All year: Peregrine falcon, raven, stonechat, rock pipit, yellowhammer, kestrel and buzzard all breed nearby; harbour porpoises may be seen. On the stable rocks and cliffs look at the lichens which characterize the different zones above the tide marks: the lowest is the black *Verrucaria maura*, which looks like tar stains; then comes the *Lecanora atra*, a grey species with dark circular scales known as black shields; next is the orange *Xanthoria parietina*, commonly called yellow scales, and finally, the pale green *Ramalina siliquosa*, or sea ivory.

14

Walk on public rights of way

Explorer 102; *Landranger* 203

By road: From St Just take B3306
S to Land's End Aerodrome. On
N side of airfield turn R on minor
road to Nanquidno. Park in small
lay-by on R at end of road before
Nanjulian Farm

SW 363 293

2 ml

2 hours

Marshy in places, otherwise
reasonable

Arable, coastal heath, scrub

Boscregan Farm SW 360 298;
burial cairns SW 357 297;
Nanjulian Farm SW 362 292;
Nanjulian beach SW 357 294;
coastal heath grazed by longhorn
cattle SW 358 295

AONB

NT

All year

Free

T: 01208 742 81 (NT, Lanhydrock)

St Just

Boscregan Farm

A visit to Boscregan Farm, near St Just, at the right time of year could leave you wondering why you hadn't heard about it or been there before. You don't need to be a naturalist to appreciate the natural beauty of this treasure.

In June and early July the fields of Boscregan Farm come to life in a wonderful blaze of colour. The arable crops grown here have a unique mix of wild flowers among them. These are rather dismissively referred to as 'arable weeds', but their beauty and value to the environment cannot be dismissed.

Well-travelled readers may be starting to link Boscregan with another site on the north coast of Cornwall – West Pentire (Site 6), where the National Trust has another arable weed project. Comparisons between the two are almost inevitable, but the differences, which include the species of flower, the methods utilized, and the unique setting, are significant. So too is the number of people who come here because, unlike West Pentire, Boscregan remains a hidden gem in the Cornish crown.

The National Trust purchased the farm as long ago as 1983, but with an inherited tenancy agreement could do little to reverse the decline in wild flowers here. In 2001 the Trust bought out the tenancy, so that they could start to manage the farm exactly as they wanted. The emphasis of the land use changed immediately from farming for profit to farming for the good of the environment. Some money is made from the barley grown here, but probably no more than to cover costs.

At Boscregan there is one flower that is found at no other site in Cornwall, and unlike many endemics it is not a shy, retiring, drab little flower hiding away

Boscregan Farm viewed from the coast path.

Corn marigolds provide a backdrop of colour at Boscregan.

in a small corner of a large field. Here, it is a bold, dark purple flower, which grows in profusion in the middle of small fields. Its expanse broken only by the statuesque, shapely nodding heads of barley and, in places, swathes of the vivid yellow corn marigolds. The contrast of dark purple and vibrant yellow is about as great as nature could possibly muster in such close proximity.

The colour purple is created by the appropriately named purple viper's bugloss. This is not the same species as the more common viper's bugloss, found in good numbers on Cornwall's sand dunes, but a

relative of it. The reason for its rarity in Britain is due to its being at the edge of its range here. More at home in a Mediterranean climate, it flourishes in warmer parts of the world. In Australia it has become a pest species after being introduced by humans, and has become known as Patterson's curse – presumably because it was taken there by someone called Patterson. The first written record of purple viper's bugloss at Boscregan was in 1873 but, considering that trading between Cornwall and mainland Europe has been taking place for millennia, it probably existed here long before.

Left: Barley and purple viper's bugloss grow side by side.
Right: The lesser snapdragon can be found growing in the arable fields at Boscregan.

It is likely that in 1873 purple viper's bugloss was more widespread in Cornwall, but instead of becoming a problem species its range has gradually contracted to this one farm, so protecting it at Boscregan is now a priority. The flower has been carefully studied here, and the effects of different farming strategies have been observed, so its requirements are now fairly well understood. Like most other arable weeds, purple viper's bugloss thrives in disturbed ground. Ploughing helps to keep its competitors at bay, and gives the flower a chance. It grows best in spring-sown arable planting, where it can at least keep up with the plants around it

View of Cape Cornwall from the beach at Nanjulian.

during the spring and early summer. Barley is grown here, since this is the traditional crop for the farm, but to assist the growth of arable weeds a four-metre margin around each field is sown with just 25 per cent of the usual barley seed, to reduce competition.

In places where the barley grows well it may be harvested to help pay for the contractors' work, but where the crop is light the seed is left for wild birds to feed on during the autumn and winter. One field on the farm is left fallow each year, to allow the birds to gain access to food for a longer period. The success of this strategy can be witnessed in the huge flocks of finches and larks visiting to feed in winter.

As at West Pentire, it is easy to be so inspired by the vibrancy of the main species of flower that we don't bother to look closer. Underneath the cover provided by the tall and colourful marigolds and bugloss is a wide range of other species – some still common, such as the scentless mayweed, redshank, scarlet pimpernel and catsear, and some increasingly rare, such as the lesser snapdragon.

The field between the coast and the farm is grazed using longhorn cattle, and is excellent for flowers in spring and summer. Hugging the coastline is an area of heath rich in heather and hummocks of wild thyme. The coast path, from which it is possible

This longhorn calf is one of the herd which graze the coast near Boscregan.

to view Boscregan Farm, passes through magical scenery, and links several fascinating archaeological sites, from the cliff castle at Nanjulian to the three cairns at Boscregan. One of the cairns contains a huge, granite boulder which was integral to the formation of the cairn, and it is thought that granite must have been highly valued by the people who made the cairn, probably in the early Bronze Age.

This is not a place that casual visitors to the county are likely to find – tucked away between tourist hot spots, it is not highly publicized, and thankfully does not have a big car-park nearby. From the small lay-by, noted in the site details, walk to the coast path, and head north for a quarter of a mile. There is a footpath leading on to the farm from here. Keep to the field edges if you wish to have a closer look at the flowers.

LOOK OUT FOR

April–June: Coastal flowers including spring squill, thrift and sea campion.

June–July: Prime time for arable weeds, particularly purple viper's bugloss and corn marigold; also scentless mayweed, redshank, catsear, scarlet pimpernel, lesser snapdragon, black mustard and prickly sow thistle; heather and wild thyme on the coastal heath. Rock samphire and sea beet nearer the sea. In the field grazed by longhorns is yellow bartsia, plenty of bird's-foot trefoil and common centaury. Common dodder on the gorse.

September–October: Best time of year for migratory birds. Look in the valley near the lay-by – a surprising number of rare birds have been seen here.

Winter: Given the policy of leaving grain in the arable fields, there are a lot of finches and larks here; the most common are chaffinch, greenfinch, linnet and skylark.

All year: Stonechat, raven, peregrine, kestrel, sparrowhawk and buzzard.

15

Walk on public rights of way
and nature reserves

Outdoor Leisure 25

By road: From Hugh Town follow
road past Porth Mellon

Lower Moors SV 912 108

5 ml (walk through nature trails
and back)

3 hours

Mostly easy walking, tricky
through Holy Vale

Wetland, open water, coastal
heath, reed-bed, woodland

Lower Moor hides SV 913 106;
Higher Moor hides SV 923 109;
Holy Vale SV 920 115;
Peninnis Head SV 912 094;
The Airfield SV 918 104;
Golf Course SV 910 120;
Watermill Cove SV 924 123;
Bar Point SV 917 129;
Old Town Church SV 912 101;
The Garrison SV 897 103

AONB, LNR, SAC, SSSI

Isles of Scilly Wildlife Trust
manages nature trails

All year

Free

T: 01720 422 153 (IoS WT)

St Mary's

The Isles of Scilly are classified as an Area of Outstanding Natural Beauty (AONB), and I don't think anyone would argue with that. Apart from their scenic value, tourists flock to the islands to enjoy their peace and quiet, as well as their wonderful beaches, clean air and beautiful gardens.

There is another reason why visitors flock to the islands, and anyone who has made the short sea crossing in autumn will know instantly to what I am referring. The vast majority of visitors to St Mary's in late September and October are twitchers. These bird-watchers, hell-bent on adding new species to their lists, book the lion's share of their annual holidays for this time of year, and migrate to the Isles of Scilly. The Scillies attract an unparalleled number of rare birds from as far afield as South East Asia and North America. Here, incredibly, it is sometimes possible to see birds from opposite sides of the earth sitting side by side in the same tree.

Twitching has become extremely well organized on the islands, and each evening during the autumn people with a keen interest in rarities meet to share their sightings. There is also a notice-board in Hugh Town giving the latest information. Often, when a rare bird is sighted on an off-island, special launches are arranged to take bird watchers to see it, which makes St Mary's an ideal base for this sort of trip. Non-twitchers should not be deterred from visiting at this time of year, because it is a good time to get to see some wonderful species, and it is easily possible to avoid the crowds – just look on the birders' board and head off in a different direction.

The island of St Mary's is the largest of the group, and has a variety of good locations for wild-

A dawn view from Peninnis Head towards Hugh Town and The Garrison.

Bar Point, St Mary's, at sunset.

life watching. For those interested in rare birds, just about any point on the island has the potential to turn up something unusual, but there are some hot spots that are always worth checking: the airfield and the golf course (for pipits, buntings and wagtails in the early morning); Penninis Head (for sea-watching and wind-blown migrants, particularly in the early morning); The Garrison (check any trees for warblers); Old Town Church (good for warblers in the trees); Bar Point (often good for sea ducks and divers in the sound), and Watermill Cove (for warblers arriving from the east).

As well as these scattered locations, there are two nature trails that pass through excellent wildlife habitats. These are called Lower Moors and Higher Moors (in which I include the extension through Holy Vale). It is easily possible to walk from Hugh Town across Lower Moors to Old Town, around the airfield along the coast path, up through Higher Moors and Holy Vale, and then return along tracks and roads to Hugh Town.

The Moors trails both have a selection of bird-watching hides overlooking wetland areas. From these, all manner of unusual birds have been seen, including waders and waterfowl. One bird that is

Top: A song thrush at Old Town churchyard.
Above: Common birds, such as the house sparrow,
are truly common on St Mary's.

the arable fields. In summer, where flowers have been harvested commercially from autumn to spring, there are a host of arable weeds, the most prolific in summer being corn marigolds, known locally as 'bothams'. Other species found in the sandy soil include the Babbington's leeks, which, at about two metres tall, tower over everything else; the nationally rare, but locally common, balm-leaved figwort; Western ramping-fumitory; the small-flowered catchfly, and the descriptively named rough-fruited buttercup, are but a few.

It is unlikely that casual visitors to St Mary's will see any mammals, because there are not many here. The only native is the Scilly shrew (lesser white-toothed shrew), which is endemic. The other two possible species are both introduced: one is the brown rat, and the other the hedgehog. Neither of these introduced mammals is particularly welcome, because both can have a devastating impact on ground-nesting birds. In environmentally sensitive areas such as around seabird colonies, rats are controlled.

For those who want to see the island at its most colourful, a visit in May or June would be ideal. This is also the best time for catching up with the island's seabirds. The most appealing seabirds do not nest on the main islands, but on the many scattered islets around the archipelago. St Mary's is a good base for exploring the smaller islands, with numerous boat

easier to see here than anywhere else that I have ever come across is the jack snipe, often recorded here from autumn through to spring. Plants growing in the marshes include royal fern, greater tussock sedge, and purple loosestrife, all of which look good in late summer. The heavily wooded area of Holy Vale is the most sheltered spot on the island, so migrant warblers such as yellow-browed warbler and firecrest often spend longer here than anywhere else.

One aspect of natural history on St Mary's which I feel is often overlooked, because of the extraordinarily high level of bird-watching interest, is the flowers of

The best way to see a puffin in Cornwall is on a boat trip from St Mary's.

trips each day. Two outings are a must for the interested naturalist: one around Annet, to see the puffins, and the evening trip to see the shearwaters, which also often visits the puffins.

Annet is home to the largest population of puffins in South West England. The colourful bill and comical attitude of the puffin make it one of Cornwall's most charismatic birds. I have always found it fascinating to watch puffins as they bring beaks full of sand-eels for their young. They are only able to collect more than

one sand-eel because they have a long, barbed tongue with which they can hold their previous catch while taking hold of the next one. They also have an extra jawbone to enable their mandibles to open in parallel.

As lovable as the puffins are, the 100 or so that breed on Annet are dwarfed in conservation value by the internationally important numbers of storm petrels that also breed here. The 3,000–4,000 petrels live in burrows alongside the puffins and several hundred Manx shearwaters.

Above: Manx shearwaters nest on Annet, and can be seen on boat trips from St Mary's.
Right: Hedgehogs can often be seen on St Mary's, particularly if camping on The Garrison.

day far out at sea, building up reserves of fat to see it through its next period of incubation. Although they are wonderful fliers when at sea, they are not very good close to land, and they are useless at walking, so returning to their burrows puts them in danger of attack from great black-backed gulls. By returning in complete darkness they are a little safer, so as the sun sets, hundreds of Manx shearwaters gather together in 'rafts', waiting for the right time to come back to land.

The reason for organizing the shearwater trip in the evening is that these mystical birds come to shore only at night. The two birds in a pair take it in turns to sit on their single egg in the darkness and safety of their burrow. While one sits, the other spends the

---

LOOK OUT FOR

May–June: Migrant birds usually include 'overshoots' from the Mediterranean, such as golden oriole, wood-chat shrike and hoopoe, as well as all the more regular British species. Basking sharks often seen between the islands.

May–July: Seabirds such as puffin, Manx shearwater, storm petrel, kittiwake, tern, shag, guillemot and razorbill are at their colonies. Flowers on the coastline are a spectacle. On the heaths look for adder's tongue fern, orange bird's-foot, dwarf pansy, milkwort and lousewort. Oystercatcher and ringed plover are the two species of wader that regularly nest on the island.

June–July: Arable weeds in the flower fields at their most prolific. Unusual insects include the Scilly bee and oil beetle.

July–September: Heather, bell heather and western gorse.

September–October: Best time for rare birds. Just about anything can be seen here, but be prepared to queue up to see the more popular rarities!

October–November: Look for black redstart on the rocky beaches.

All year: Grey seal. Common birds such as linnet, song thrush, house sparrow and robin are present in great densities.

16

Walk on public rights of way

Outdoor Leisure 25

SV 887 154

5 ml

5 hours

Difficult and rocky to N of island, easy to S

Heathland, woodland, lake, reed-bed, sand dune, cliff, beach

Garden entrance SV 893 142;
New Grimsby Quay SV 887 154;
Old Grimsby SV 894 156;
Cromwell's Castle SV 882 159

AONB, SAC

All year

T: 01720 422 536
(IoS Tourist Information Centre);
www.scillyonline.co.uk

Tresco

Tresco is probably the most famous of the Isles of Scilly – a fact due in part to it having one of our best-known gardens. To create the garden, many thousands of plant specimens have been acquired from around the world by the Dorrien Smith family, who have owned the island since the 1830s. Their work in maintaining the gardens, together with the various forms of agriculture on the island, have ensured that there are a great many different habitats for wildlife in a relatively small area.

The island can be split into its habitat types. In the north is an area of waved heath, surrounded by a rocky shore with only a few beaches; the central region consists of a mixture of small fields and hedgerows used for both flower-growing and rearing livestock; further south, adjacent to the house and formal gardens, are two lakes, known as the Great and Abbey pools, while around the shore at the south end of the island, particularly to the south-east, is an extensive system of dunes and beautiful white beaches.

For a walk around Tresco I will start at New Grimsby, which is the usual landing point for day visitors to the island unless the tide is low. Heading north along the coast soon brings us to Cromwell's Castle. The narrow strip of coast between the path and the sea is good for the usual mix of spring flowers, such as thrift and sea campion, and inland of the path is a classic example of waved heath. The dominant plant here is heather, but there is also bird's-foot trefoil, and swathes of honeysuckle can be seen in sheltered spots.

Nesting on the small cliffs at the north end of the island are kittiwakes. Listen for the 'kitti-waaaake' call – this is quite obvious once you are aware of it, but the amalgamation of sound created by a few

The Abbey Gardens, Tresco.

Cromwell's Castle, Tresco.

Scilly bee and several types of solitary bee. Peregrine falcons may be spotted here, since they nest on the rocky islet to the north of Tresco called Men-a-vaur.

Continuing the clockwise circumnavigation of the island soon brings us to Old Grimsby. Nesting under the eaves and windowsills of several houses are some of the most easily watched house martins I have ever seen. In summer it is a real privilege to be able to watch them almost at eye level as they fly back and forth with mud for nest-building or food for their young.

While walking along the east side of the island, particularly around the blockhouse, don't forget to look out into the channel between here and St Martin's. The islands in this channel, as well as the one between Tresco and Bryher, are among the best nest sites on the Scillies for terns.

Terns resemble small, nimble gulls; they nest in colonies and are very noisy, particularly when defending their colony from predation by gulls. The state of the tern colonies on the Scillies has come under close scrutiny recently, because the islands were once home to the very rare roseate tern. This species bred on the Scillies as recently as the 1990s, and since it is a target species of the UK Biodiversity Action Plan (BAP), instated in response to the 1992 Rio Earth Summit, the Scillies have been named as one of five sites in which we should aim to have roseate terns breeding again in the future.

In recent years the breeding terns have been closely monitored by the Isles of Scilly Wildlife Trust, so that it can be clear about the factors that might cause the success or failure of their nests and young. It has become apparent that the terns are very mobile, and make their nests in different places each year, choosing from a total of about 20 popular breeding sites. It seems there is plenty of food for the adults to bring back to their young, and that predation of their eggs and chicks, by gulls and rats, is no higher than would normally be expected.

dozen birds can be confusing. The kittiwake is a gull, but it has a buoyant flight reminiscent of a tern; its black wing-tips show very little white in them, and look as if they have been dipped in ink.

Inhabiting the gorse and taller stands of heather are several pairs of stonechats, which flick from perch to perch in search of insects. On a calm day there are many insects here, drawn by the nectar of the flowers on the heath. Insect species that may be found include the common blue and small copper butterflies, and a wide variety of bees, including the

A pair of kittiwakes displaying.

Two factors that have been of greater significance to the terns here are related to weather and people. In recent years large colonies of common terns have been devastated by an unfortunate combination of high tide and stormy weather in June – a fact which might be indicative of climate change, or just bad luck. The other significant problem experienced by terns is disturbance on their breeding grounds. They nest on shingle beaches and maritime heathland, which are just the sorts of places that people like to visit in the summer. One of the main strategies employed in assisting the terns is to fence off breeding areas in places likely to be subjected to disturbance; another has involved attracting terns to safe nesting areas using stereo systems playing recordings of their own calls.

After walking along the dunes, the wetland area of the Great Pool soon comes into sight. I suggest walking along the northern edge of the lake, and then back along its southern edge, because this area of standing water, with its surrounding reed-bed and tall pines, is very attractive to a wide range of breeding birds.

Typical birds of the reed bed are sedge and reed warblers which breed here in good numbers, but autumnal rarities such as penduline and bearded tits are occasionally seen. The little egrets which spend

Above: Arctic terns occasionally breed on islets around Tresco.
Right: This house martin was building a nest above a window in Old Grimsby.

their entire year around the pool have yet to start breeding, but this can only be a matter of time. In 2005 a pair of marsh harriers first stayed here to nest, which was great news because, although marsh harriers have frequently been recorded passing through Scilly, this was the first time that they have been known to breed. The Isles of Scilly Bird Group have three hides facing out on to the Great Pool, which make bird-watching comfortable.

Top: A female chaffinch drinks from the fountain in the gardens.
Above: The black redstart can be seen on the islands in autumn.

Around the pool is the largest area of mature woodland on the islands. Consisting of some quite old trees, it is home to just a few species of hole-nesting woodland birds that on mainland Cornwall we take a little for granted. Birds like blue and great tits have only nested here since the 1950s, and many others, such as the coal tit and great spotted woodpecker, have still to find a toehold here. Other birds that nest here include rook, blackcap, and grey heron, but the fact that there is so much cover for birds means that windblown birds can find shelter, and migrants often move on to Tresco from the more exposed islands of Bryher and St Martin's.

After completing the circuit of the Great Pool, the gardens are a 'must' for visitors. Their impressive range of plants, the combination of which do not and probably would not grow anywhere else in Britain, is amazing. The gardens are rich in bird life and, as always on the Scillies, the garden birds are extremely tame. The ornate fountain is the centre of attention on a hot day, when blackbirds, house sparrows, chaffinches, song thrushes and dunnocks queue to take a dip. In the bushes around the entrance to the gardens, and near the Valhalla Ship's Figurehead Museum, look carefully for stick insects – this is one of the best spots to see these alien creepy crawlies.

LOOK OUT FOR

May–June: Overshooting migrants, whose intended destination is the Mediterranean region, sometimes find their way here, often including woodchat shrike, hoopoe and golden oriole.

May–August: Swallow, house martin, cuckoo, willow warbler, sedge warbler, reed warbler, chiffchaff, black-cap – all breed on the island. The terns breeding on the small islands around Tresco are nearly all common terns (some 75 pairs). There may also be sandwich terns fishing in the area, and an odd pair of Arctic terns; there are some records of roseate terns each year, which hopefully will breed again. Kittiwakes nest on the island; marsh harriers bred for the first time in 2005 in the reed-bed at the Great Pool.

September–October: Rare birds of any type could be seen. Waders, gulls and waterfowl are attracted to the margins of the Great and Abbey Pools.

October–November: Black redstart on the beaches.

October–February: Great northern diver in the sea.

All year: Song thrush, robin, chaffinch and greenfinch are very numerous and tame.

St Martin's

I can never quite make up my mind as to which of the Isles of Scilly is my favourite, but St Martin's is always pretty high up the list. There are two reasons that make me lean towards St Martin's – its combination of white, sandy beaches and rugged headlands, and its supremely calming and peaceful nature.

The ferries from St Mary's usually drop off day visitors at Higher Town quay, so I will start my suggested walk from that point and work my way in an anticlockwise fashion around the island.

One of the first things that strikes home about bird-watching on islands is that any unusual habitat can contain something interesting. Only a few yards from the quay is a cricket square cum helicopter pad. This is the shortest mown grass you are likely to find on the island, so check it out carefully before stamping across it, there may be wagtails, pipits, larks and buntings here. Inland from this field is a small area of woodland. Small it may be, but insignificant it is not. There isn't much of this habitat on St Martin's, and these trees are quite likely to hold warblers and finches, particularly during times of migration. In fact these trees and hedges are where a great deal of the mist-netting and ringing of birds is carried out on the island. At the end of the cricket field is a small pond. If this were on the mainland, you wouldn't give it a second look, but on an island miss it at your peril – the first time I visited St Martin's, in May, there was a tired Squacco heron fishing in here.

The first headland on this route is called English Island Point, and from here it is possible to look out over the uninhabited islets and rocks of the Eastern Isles. Seabirds and seals may be seen in the channel here, and breeding on the rocky islands there may

Thrift growing on English Island Point with Higher Town Bay.

Sanderlings visit the sandy beaches of St Martin's in the autumn and winter.

also be a pair of ravens, which sometimes fly around this tip of St Martin's.

The Day Mark – a tower built to aid shipping around the islands – can be clearly seen from here, and is the next obvious target. On top of Chapel Down, around the Day Mark, is a classic area of waved heath, where the heather is interspersed with bird's-foot trefoil and thrift, while growing on most of the stems and bare ground is a profusion of lichens. Over the years gorse and bracken have been encroaching on to this heath. The Isles of Scilly Wildlife Trust is tackling the problem by rolling and cutting the bracken and burning the gorse, so don't be alarmed to see burnt patches. As you walk by it is interesting to look at the recovery rate of different species after a burn.

Continuing around the edge of the island, after passing a couple of small, sandy beaches we come to Turfy Hill. Unfortunately, this particular spot has been invaded by an unusual and unwanted plant, a species of phormium known as New Zealand Flax. This plant was introduced on to the island because it was thought that it might be useful in making ropes,

Left: Oystercatchers nest around the island.
Right: A ringed plover among the flowers at The Cove, St Martin's.

and certainly its leaves seem to have the right qualities, but that hope was never realized, and instead this phormium has started to dominate the landscape and local flora. The Wildlife Trust is tackling the problem by removing the plants' flower heads each year to stop it spreading, and by cutting it back where it obstructs paths.

Ahead lies one of the most wonderful sights on Scilly – the beautiful white beaches of Great and Little Bays, backed by the rocks of Scilly Point and White Island. This is a fantastic place, though I prefer it out of season when I can have it to myself – except for the sanderlings and turnstones which frequent the beaches from October through the winter.

White Island is a tidal island cut off from St Martin's at high tide, so be careful if you wish to take a walk over. It has a greater density of breeding waders than on St Martin's because it is quieter, so be sensitive to their needs, and don't keep them off their nests in summer. The two waders that you are likely to encounter are the oystercatcher, which will certainly let you know if you disturb it, and the ringed plover, whose behaviour is much more subtle. Walk too close to a ringed plover's nest and it will run on

Left: The view from St Martin's Head across to St Martin's Bay.
Above: The oil beetle is a distinctive species of the coastal grassland on St Martin's.

ahead of you, to lead you away, often pretending to be injured by hanging a wing at its side.

At the crossing point to White Island is a gorgeous piece of maritime heath. People have played here for centuries, making mazes out of pebbles from the beach and ropes washed up from ships. The effect of feet, wind and salt spray keeps the grass in check, and provides an environment in which flowers can grow. The only other habitat that I have ever seen which resembles this is the machair (an extensive low-lying fertile plain) of the Outer Hebrides, and that is world famous for its density of common but colourful flowers. Here on St Martin's we have the fiery yellow bird's-foot trefoil, purple heather, lemon yellow of the lady's bedstraw, orange bird's-foot, the white of both eyebright and heath bedstraw, together with the deep pink of thrift and pale pink of English stonecrop. Clinging to the stones, preventing their actual surface from being seen, is a whole host of lichens of different statures, colours and shapes.

Continuing along the north-west coast of St Martin's, watch out for another locally important species, the oil beetle – in May and June they are exceptionally common along the path here. This

The wren is found commonly on the islands.

noted in the wren population: there is a species called the Scilly bee, and even the speckled wood butterflies appear, to me, to be bigger and more colourful than their mainland counterparts. There is no doubt that the male blackbirds on the Scillies have much more colourful beaks than those in Cornwall. Whether this is genetic or dietetic is not fully understood, but it might be that by foraging for insects among the decaying seaweed of the islands' beaches they pick up more of one particular mineral than typical blackbirds on the mainland.

From Lower Town Quay I usually walk back along the road to Higher Town. This way I can visit a tearoom or shop along the way.

strangely shaped beetle has a blue-black body with a huge abdomen and beaded antennae. Inland from here is an area of gorse and scrub behind the public house, which can be good in May for some unusual rarities such as the golden oriole.

The Lower Town Quay is situated opposite another nearby island known as Tean. This island, like the heaths of St Martin's, used to be grazed by cattle and, when it was, its short turf was an excellent place for wild flowers. Living on the island was a population of common blue butterflies. Because of their separation from others of their kind they developed different characteristics – in particular, they were larger than other common blues, even those found on St Martin's.

This is not the only example of evolution working to create differences between island and mainland wildlife. Slight differences in appearance have been

---

LOOK OUT FOR

May: Mediterranean birds arriving here accidentally include golden oriole, woodchat shrike and Squacco heron.

June–July: The waved heathland around the Day Mark is at its best. Special flowers found here include adder's-tongue fern, western clover, tormentil and dwarf pansies. Insects include species of solitary bee, the Scilly bee, and red barbed ant (known at only two other sites in the UK); oil beetles are a feature of the grassy areas. Nesting waders include oystercatcher and ringed plover; fulmars nest around the coast, and terns may be seen fishing, particularly along the sandy southern shore; recently a pair of nightjars bred on the island. The flowers in the area close to the causeway over to White Island are beautiful, with orange bird's-foot a specialty.

September–October: Due to St Martin's location to the north-east of the island group, many migrant birds arriving from the east make their first landfall here, including red-breasted flycatcher, wryneck, Pallas's and yellow-browed warbler. Look out for sanderling on the beaches.

of location	Walk on public rights of way
map	*Explorer* 102; *Landranger* 203
rections to start point	By road: From Penzance W on A30 towards Land's End; turn L on B3283, signed to St Buryan and Minack theatre. Keep following signs to Minack; drive past its entrance along minor road from Porthcurno to St Levan. Park in field just before church on R
rting point	Parking available in Porthgwarra SW 371 218, but for suggested walk park by church in St Levan SW 381 223
length	Approx 3 ml
nded time	3 hours (for sea-watching and migrant-spotting)
conditions	Rocky and difficult walking
habitats	Coastal heath, scrub
of interest	Gwennap Head SW 367 215; St Levan Church SW 381 223; Porthgwarra Cove SW 371 218 (shop, lavatories)
esignation	AONB
te facilities	*Note:* Light refreshments at shop

Porthgwarra

Look at Cornwall on a map, and you see that it is at the far south-west of Britain, so maybe the extreme south-westerly point on the mainland is as Cornish as Cornwall gets. The most south-westerly point is not the over-developed and over-visited Land's End complex, but the much quieter, quainter and more Cornish Gwennap Head, together with its adjacent fishing cove and hamlet of Porthgwarra.

If geography is ever important in determining the nature of a place, then it certainly is here. There is nothing, except the Isles of Scilly, between here and America, and the headland is regularly pounded by gales and lashed by the ocean. The short vegetation of Gwennap Head is dominated by stunted heather forming a waved heath which, moulded by the wind, mimics the shape of the sea. Even the hard Cornish granite here is at the mercy of the elements, with every weakness in its core exploited by the erosive powers of water and wind, creating sculpted forms of captivating beauty. Every surface, whether of rock, heather or bare ground is smothered in lichen, indicative of the cleanliness of the atmosphere and the slow rate of change in this environment.

Though the vegetation can seem timeless, the seasons bring with them their own subtle changes to the colour of the valley. In spring the more sheltered parts of the area come to life with the vibrant yellow of gorse, with its heavenly coconut scent. A couple of months later, this same gorse which so dominated the landscape will itself be dominated by the parasitic plant known as common dodder. This alien-looking species spreads itself like a tangled web over the gorse, and draws from its host all of the nutrients it requires.

The hamlet of Porthgwarra nestles beneath Gwennap Head.

Above: Common dodder is a parasitic plant often completely smothering its host plant, gorse.
Right: Navelwort grows on rocks and walls.

The flowers among the rocks on the slopes down to the sea include all of the species typical of the Cornish coastline, but growing on the rocks and from cracks in the granite hedges you will find navelwort, sometimes known as 'wall pennywort'. This is a succulent plant related to the stonecrops; its circular leaves and long green flower spikes make this one of Cornwall's most characteristic plants.

The headland attracts most interest from bird-watchers in late summer and autumn, when the geographical position of Porthgwarra really becomes significant. Birds carried by the Gulf Stream from America make their first landfall here, and birds coming from the east, for whatever reason, are funnelled to a point as they fly south and west along our peninsula. At first light, migrants can be found anywhere on the headland, but later in the day many move down to the shelter of the valley where there are trees and bushes. The best months for migrant-watching are September and October, but May can

The great skua is one of many species of seabird that might be seen from Gwennap Head in the autumn.

also be rewarding. To try to list the species that might be seen here would be futile: expect the unexpected, and don't be afraid to ask what people are looking at.

Birds are not restricted to living on land, so to a birder the pastime of sea-watching is much more than simply gazing out to sea enjoying the rollers and breakers; it opens up a whole new kind of bird-watching. Bird-watchers bring binoculars and telescopes here on the windiest of days, to huddle behind rocks on Gwennap Head and scan the sea for birds. From August to October they are looking for seabirds blown closer to land than normal by strong south-westerly winds. Birds that are very rarely seen from any other British headland are sometimes seen from Gwennap Head. Classically these include great, Cory's and Mediterranean shearwaters, and Arctic, long-tailed, pomarine and great skuas.

The sea here plays host to more than just birds, and this is as good a place as any to see dolphins, porpoises, and even whales and sharks. The species seen here, in a roughly declining order of frequency, include harbour porpoise, bottlenose dolphin, common dolphin, pilot whale and Risso's dolphin. Visit in June and there is a better than average chance of seeing a basking shark here. Indeed, they are often seen anywhere from the Lizard to Gwennap Head, and less frequently along the north coast up to Bude. Basking sharks are relatively easy to find if the sea is calm, because they swim with their dorsal fin protruding from the water. Look for them in areas of the sea that have a different surface texture. Such areas, where the underwater current rises, are rich in plankton. Unlike the great white shark of *Jaws* fame, the basking shark is a plankton-eater, so perfectly harmless to humans.

There is parking in Porthgwarra, but for a pleasant walk park behind the church at St Levan, and then walk along the coast path to Porthgwarra Cove. The cove itself is an attractive, small fishing harbour with an unusual walk-through tunnel leading down to the slipway. It is said that this tunnel was cut to allow farmers to collect seaweed from the beach using carts.

Left: The rocky slipway and cave-like tunnel allow access to the sea at Porthgwarra Cove.
Above: In summer whitethroats are seen in the scrub.
Above right: Basking sharks are most frequently seen between here and the east side of the Lizard in June.

The coast path from here leads west around Gwennap Head. This was once the main Coastguard communication centre for the Land's End area, but was subsumed within the newer Falmouth Coastguard office in the early 1980s. The lookout is still manned on a voluntary basis by the National Coastwatch Institution, and the view from here during a south-westerly storm is, frankly, awesome. The two conical structures on the headland mark the direction of the Runnelstone, a dangerous reef hidden just below the surface of the sea; beyond the reef is the Runnelstone Buoy, with a hydrophone that makes a hauntingly eerie sound audible from Porthgwarra on a calm day. After walking around the headland return to the cove and back along the coast path.

LOOK OUT FOR

April–May: Flowers include primrose, lousewort, sea campion, thrift, gorse and spring squill. Migrant birds frequently include common birds such as wheatear, and sometimes 'overshoots' from the continent, such as woodchat shrike and hoopoe.

June–July: Flowers such as English stonecrop, sheep's-bit scabious, wild carrot, wild thyme, bird's-foot trefoil, red campion and heathspotted orchid. Growing on the gorse look for common dodder, and on rocks and walls for navelwort. Breeding birds include sedge warbler, stonechat, raven, meadow pipit, skylark, whitethroat, kestrel and peregrine. At sea look for basking shark.

September–October: The most frequent rarities are, from the east, wryneck, red-breasted flycatcher and yellow-browed warbler; there may also be barred warbler and bluethroat. From the west, various New World warblers. Commoner migrants include chiffchaff, pied flycatcher, blackcap, meadow pipit, skylark and wood pigeon.

All year: The best spot in Cornwall for watching cetaceans; sightings have included common dolphin, bottlenose dolphin, harbour porpoise, minke whale, Risso's dolphin and pilot whale.

location	Nature reserve
map	*Explorer* 102; *Landranger* 203
directions to start point	By road: From A30 S of Hayle take turn to Marazion at next roundabout. Turn L at T-junction, then first L into minor road. Park on R
starting point	SW 513 312
size	53 ha/133 a
length	3 ml, includes walking on to marsh and across causeway
estimated time	3 hours
conditions	Reserve can get wet; otherwise good walking conditions
habitats	Marsh, reed-bed, beach, sand-dune
interest	Causeway to Mount SW 516 304; viewing point over standing water SW 506 314; viewing point for starling roost SW 510 312
designation	AONB, SSSI
owner	RSPB
open	All year (guided walks in summer)
entry	Free
enquiries	T: 01736 711 682 (Marazion Marsh)
facilities	

Marazion Marsh

Marazion Marsh reserve has the largest area of reeds in Cornwall; recorded within its boundaries have been a staggering 500 plant species; 250 insects, and 250 birds, so its potential for attracting wildlife is obvious.

Apart from providing a home to an impressive list of species, Marazion also plays host to one of Cornwall's most spectacular natural history phenomena – the starling roost. If you have never seen a big starling roost then you probably won't believe how awe-inspiring it can be. Starlings fly from all over the surrounding countryside, arriving in small groups of maybe a few thousand each. On a good night they stay in the air awaiting the arrival of other birds. Gradually, the overall flock size builds up to 100,000 or more starlings. Swirling in the sky like a shoal of fish in the ocean, they seem to enjoy putting on a show for astonished onlookers, but in fact they are gathering for safety. Occasionally, when a sparrowhawk flies among them hoping for an easy snack, the reaction of the flock serves to confuse and frustrate the hapless bird of prey. When the starlings decide to come down to settle for the night they funnel out of the sky like a tornado into the reed-bed.

The most crucial factor when timing a visit to see the starling roost is the time of year. Numbers peak in late autumn and winter, so I would suggest that November is the best month. There is no point arriving early in the day because the birds arrive just as the sun is setting. The best view is from the coast road, though for photography it might be better to go into the reserve and look back against the setting sun.

Of the birds that breed on the reserve, the most significant is the Cetti's warbler. Unlike most other

The marsh at Marazion has the largest reed-bed in Cornwall.

warblers, this one is a resident species. It is very shy, even for a warbler, and lives in reed-beds, particularly where willow and scrub encroach. The Cetti's warbler is not a very colourful bird, it is simply pale brown underneath and slightly darker brown on top, but it does have a rather colourful song. A sudden, explosive array of high-pitched notes from a bush in the reed-bed is enough to clinch a Cetti's warbler. To optimize your chances of hearing one, visit in early spring and in the early morning.

Other breeding birds here include reed warbler, sedge warbler, reed bunting, and grey heron – in fact this is Cornwall's only colony of ground-nesting grey herons. During August and September Marazion Marsh regularly plays host to two very rare migrants. The aquatic warbler and spotted crake are seen here more frequently than anywhere else in the county, though they occur in only small numbers and are both quite elusive.

The aquatic warbler shows a distinct preference for the beds of glaucous bulrush close to the entrance to the reserve. Of the other birds found at Marazion, the aquatic warbler is only likely to be confused with the sedge warbler. The key difference is that it has a cream crown stripe as well as the two cream stripes over the eyes of the sedge warbler, but be careful when identifying one because young sedge warblers can look very similar. Check the information panel in the small car-park, because news of the latest sightings is usually posted here.

Intensive work has been carried out on this particular reserve in recent years to make it more appealing to bitterns. Bitterns like reed-beds that contain plenty of standing water, and channels in which to fish, so at Marazion long ditches are cut through the reeds on a five-yearly cycle. So far bitterns have only been recorded during the winter, but even if they don't stay to breed here, the contribution that Marazion makes to their survival can still be significant.

Top: The Cetti's warbler is a rare breeding bird at Marazion Marsh.
Above: This snow bunting spent a winter feeding around the high tide-line of the beach.
Right: The starling roost at Marazion is the most amazing bird spectacle in Cornwall.

Above: The causeway to the Mount is an excellent place from which to watch waders.
Left: One of a small group of purple sandpipers that can usually be found on the beach in winter.
Right: These curlews were roosting on Chapel Rock at Marazion beach.

If you visit the marsh to watch birds, then don't overlook the nearby beach. Just over the road from the reserve car-park is a small area of sand dunes, and continuing along towards Marazion there is the famous causeway to St Michael's Mount. The edge of the dunes, and even the beach near the main Marazion car-park, are good for larks, wagtails, pipits and buntings in autumn and winter.

The causeway is a good place from which to watch waders, partly because it allows easy access across the sand and rocks, but also because birds become accustomed to people crossing here. If you

flaged against the rocks and seaweed. Fortunately, they are one of our most approachable wading birds. Look for them as the tide reaches its height – this way they have fewer places to hide!

can get close to a flock of small waders on the rocks here, then it will consist of just three species: dunlin, turnstone, and purple sandpiper. The most nervous of these birds are the dunlin, and if you cause them to fly then the rest are likely to go with them, so take your time, and approach with caution. Keep your outline as small as possible, and when you sense a nervousness in the flock sit or crouch down, then either wait for them to come to you (forced back by the tide), or move very slowly.

This is one of only a few sites in the county where it is possible to see the purple sandpiper, the plumage of which is hardly as colourful as its name might suggest. The 'purple' sandpiper is actually a sooty brown colour, which makes it extremely well camou-

LOOK OUT FOR

February–March: Listen for a Cetti's warbler.

March–April: Garganey often seen on passage; grey heron breeds.

April–May: Migrant birds include common and sandwich terns at sea, and whimbrel on the beach. On the reserve look for ragged robin, flag iris and hemlock water dropwort.

June–August: The pools of the reserve are good for dragonflies. The 14 species recorded here include common hawker, black-tailed skimmer, and the rare red-veined darter. Flowers include marsh woundwort, purple loosestrife, meadowsweet and skullcap on the marsh, and sea holly on the beach. Breeding birds include reed warbler, sedge warbler and reed bunting.

August–September: Possible aquatic warbler and spotted crake; swallows and martins roost overnight in the reed-bed.

October–November: Look for snow bunting and black redstart on the strandline.

Autumn–Winter: The fantastic starling roost is a 'must see'. Gulls, often including glaucous and Mediterranean, can be seen on the beach or bathing on the open water of the reserve. Ducks, such as teal, wigeon, shoveler and gadwall, are at their most numerous: look for them on the reserve from the coast road; ducks on the sea have included eider, common scoter, velvet scoter, and even king eider and surf scoter; there may also be great northern divers.

Winter: Look for waders on the beach, including sanderling, dunlin, turnstone, ringed plover, purple sandpiper, curlew, oystercatcher, grey plover and little egret; jack snipe are usually recorded here.

20

Walk on public rights of way

Explorer 102; *Landranger* 203

By road: From Hayle take B3302 to Leedstown; turn R on B3280 to Townshend, then L; approx 1 ml car-park signed to R

SW 600 321

220 ha/550 a

Approx 4 ml

3 hours

Some rough walking, some muddy paths

Heath, hill, mixed woodland, mining waste, river

Main car-park SW 600 321; alternative car-parks SW 600 324, SW 596 307; Godolphin Hill SW 593 313; tin-streaming area SW 600 324; woodland with paths SW 604 323

AGLV, SSSI

NT

All year

Free

T: 01736 762 479

Pub in Godolphin Cross

Godolphin

The estate around Godolphin House has been owned by the National Trust since 2000. Major changes have taken place there since then, the most significant of which have been to improve access for people around the woods and on Godolphin Hill. Wildlife habitats are also being revitalized, so this is now a very rewarding area for exploration.

There are three distinct types of habitat around the Godolphin estate. Probably the most impressive is the hill with its heathland (and marvellous views). There is also the highly regarded woodland, with a fine showing of bluebells, and finally there is possibly the least promising but actually most highly protected area of the estate around the River Hayle, between the woods and Godolphin Bridge, which is dominated by a dry heath growing on mining waste.

The hill was becoming distinctly overgrown until the Trust began a process of rolling bracken and cutting gorse. By opening up pathways, the Trust has been able to introduce a herd of Shetland ponies that graze from March to July, or thereabouts. These ponies are very friendly, and certainly nothing to fear. They ignore dogs and people alike, just getting on with the business of grazing rough grass, chewing at gorse and trampling bracken. The transformation brought about by their efforts has been amazing. Not only can walkers gain access to the hill from four sides, but the edges of the paths in spring are alive with flowers. The two most notable species of flower to have benefited from the management are wood anemone and wood sorrel, but bluebells also grow on the hill, and it can only be a matter of time before heath spotted orchids show their heads again.

There is obviously a balance to be struck between access and wildlife. Some of the gorse, bracken and

A mist hangs in the woods around Godolphin.

blackthorn will have to be left in place to cater for an important population of breeding birds. One of the most notable of these is the cuckoo. Usually arriving mid- to late April, these birds make themselves noticed until their early departure in summer. On still mornings and evenings through spring and summer, grasshopper warblers can be heard reeling – a sound reminiscent of a persistent grasshopper. Stonechats and linnets are always numerous, nesting in the gorse, and reed buntings are present in small numbers during the summer.

The only point higher than Godolphin Hill in the surrounding area is Tregonning Hill, to the south, so the panoramic view including St Ives, Carn Brea, Helston, Mount's Bay and Trencrom is impressive. Since this hill is so dominant in the landscape it acts as a significant beacon for migratory birds, and is a good place to watch for them. A couple of the regular highlights include occasional merlin in the

Left: A view from Godolphin Hill at sunset.
Top: This male cuckoo spends its summers on Godolphin Hill.
Above: This foal was born on the hill.

Left: The Cladonia floerkeana *is thankfully better known as the matchstick lichen.*
Right: The purple hairstreak can be seen well at Godolphin among the stunted oak trees.

autumn, and flocks of golden plover in the winter, but anything is possible.

The footpath from the hill down towards the house passes through a line of trees in which you may see spotted flycatchers during the summer. Fail here and there is a good chance of seeing them in the woodland. As the surroundings change to a mixture of farmland and mature trees, so the chance of seeing mistle thrush, great spotted woodpecker and jay increases. Around the house is an area of woodland renowned for its bluebells in late April and early May. Much of this is still privately owned, so access is limited. The woodlands on the other side of the minor road between Townshend and Godolphin Cross have plenty of footpaths which can be used to lead down to the River Hayle.

The river is quite small, and has been heavily manipulated in the past. Tin streaming has been carried out here, and piles of waste materials are still in evidence along the valley bottom. Human influence has created unusual habitats for wildlife. Where ground is left bare and plants fail to germinate, we see mosses and lichens growing. This area has been designated a Site of Special Scientific Interest (SSSI) because of its rare liverworts and mosses: it has six species which are classified as either nationally rare or scarce – for example, *Cephaloziella nicholsonii*, a minute liverwort found only in Cornwall, Devon and Cheshire. In winter, look out for the spore capsules of mosses growing up to form miniature jungles, and the striking red-fruiting bodies of the lichen *Cladonia floerkeana*, often known as the matchstick lichen.

The river is not particularly rich in life, since it is quite steeply banked and fast flowing, but it does play host to two distinctive species of dragonfly, the beautiful demoiselle and the golden-ringed dragonfly. The trees and scrub in the valley are obviously appealing to birds, since they always attract whitethroats, blackcaps and willow warblers to breed. I have had the pleasure of seeing numerous firecrests here in the winter, as well as a wryneck one autumn, and a long-eared owl one winter.

The pools of freestanding water, created by the river flooding in winter, are occupied by frogs and toads looking for somewhere to spawn. The shorter areas of grass are interspersed with flowers such as English stonecrop, self-heal and ground ivy, while the longer grass is colonized by lesser stitchwort, foxglove and red campion. Green woodpeckers are common – they like the mixture of pine trees and short grass.

Many of the trees growing on the ground disturbed by tin-streaming are dwarfed through the contamination of the soil by heavy metals. But even this has its benefits, because the woods of Godolphin are regarded as one of the best places in Cornwall to see the purple hairstreak butterfly – not a rare creature, but because it lives and feeds in the tops of mature oak trees, it is not always easy to spot.

The whole area can easily be covered on foot from the main car-park, where there are laminated maps available to carry around. An assortment of circular routes can be planned to encompass the different habitats. Be aware that the path coming down through farmland to the north of the hill crosses pasture which is often used by a herd of very playful cattle. Other than that, there is nothing to fear, and plenty to gain from a walk around Godolphin Estate.

Earthballs are common on bare ground near the river.

LOOK OUT FOR

January–March: Gorse in flower by the river and on the hill.

April–May: Wood sorrel and wood anemone on the hill; bluebells in the woods; good for ferns in the woodland, including common polypody, hard fern and hartstongue fern.

May–June: Listen for grasshopper warbler and cuckoo on the hill.

June–August: Beautiful demoiselle and golden-ringed dragonfly by the river. Purple hairstreak butterfly best seen on smaller oak trees.

Summer: Spotted flycatcher, willow warbler, whitethroat and reed bunting.

October–November: Fungi in the woods include sulphur tuft, shaggy ink cap, honey fungus, King Alfred's cakes, jelly antler fungus, Jew's ear, amethyst deceiver, and jelly babies. Fungi under the pine trees on the mining waste include common earthball, fragile russula and rufus milkcap. It is worth looking for merlin on the hill.

Winter: Firecrest in the pine trees between wood and river. Lichens, mosses and liverworts by the river.

All year: Green woodpecker, great spotted woodpecker, nuthatch, sparrowhawk, buzzard, blackcap, chiffchaff, stonechat and linnet.

location	Walk on public rights of way
map	*Explorer* 103; *Landranger* 203
ctions to art point	By road: In Helston take B3304 towards Porthleven. At end of boating lake is free car-park on L
ng point	SW 654 268
length	6 ml
ded time	4 hours
onditions	Mostly good footpaths, some parts wet in winter
habitats	Woodland, lake, wetland, willow carr, pebble beach, reed-bed
f interest	Loe Bar SW 643 242; Degibna Woods SW 649 250; hide SW 647 256; Penrose Estate SW 644 257
signation	AONB, SSSI
owner	NT owns much of the land
open	All year
entry	Free
enquiries	T: 01208 742 81 (NT, Lanhydrock)
facilities	*Note:* Wheelchair access limited to N edge of lake. Do not allow dogs to drink the water. Refreshments and lavatories at boating lake

Loe Pool

Climate change is rarely out of the news today, but it is certainly not a recent phenomenon. Loe Pool, near Helston, would not be here today if it wasn't for climate change. Its formation was caused by the raising of sea levels after the last Ice Age, approximately 10,000 years ago. The encroaching sea brought with it a mass of shingle, and dumped it between two cliffs at the mouth of the River Cober. The flow of the river was effectively blocked, and the pool started to fill. The bar, which became known as Loe Bar, is technically a barrier beach because it is permanently above sea level.

People with knowledge of the history of Cornish place-names will know that the name Loe Pool is unnecessarily repetitious, since the word *loe* is derived from *loch* – a word whose roots are firmly established in Celtic soil. It is likely that the lake used to be known simply as The Loe.

Starting the circular walk of the pool from Helston, a choice of paths alongside the River Cober leads to the main track along the western edge of the lake. In this grassy area are a couple of pools which are home to several species of dragonfly in summer, as well as the usual mallards and swans. Along the river it may be possible to see kingfishers, but it is best to arrive early, before they are disturbed by other walkers. Through autumn and winter, this is a good place to see flocks of siskin feeding in the alders – these yellow and black finches favour wetland areas.

Soon you will reach the lake where, in autumn and winter, there are plenty of diving ducks and one or two grebes. A hide can be found down a small path to the left, which is a good place to stop to have a look over the water. From here look for wildfowl – typically tufted duck, gadwall, pochard and

Loe Bar at sunset.

Above: Gadwall are common on the lake in winter (left). Coots are always active on the lake (right). Left: Siskins, such as this male, can be seen here in the winter.

little grebe, but there may be pintail and shoveler among others.

The hedge banks alongside this path are a sight in spring when the red, white and blue of red campion, greater stitchwort and bluebells combine to great patriotic effect. Pause for a while overlooking the inlet at Penrose Estate, this is another good spot for birds. Grey herons sometimes feed at the water's edge, and ducks usually gather here. In spring look out for cuckoo flower in the wet meadow.

The stretch of path between Penrose and the coast is excellent for butterflies, particularly in mid-summer, with small tortoiseshell, peacock and red

Cormorants readily take to fresh-water lakes, and there are always plenty around Loe Pool.

admiral all common. In early summer I have also seen small pearl-bordered fritillary here. Resting on the branches of dead trees at the water's edge there will be many cormorants with their wings held out to dry. This prehistoric bird is often encountered at inland waterways, unlike its close relative, the shag, which is almost exclusively coastal in its distribution.

September is a good time for seeing birds passing through. If you are very lucky there might even be an osprey joining the cormorants in their quest for fish, though their hunting technique is somewhat more elaborate and impressive. Fish in the lake include perch, rudd, brown trout, and an unusual form of sea trout which has evolved separately through its isolation from others of its type by the bar.

In summer the bar comes to life with unusual flowers. The lack of organic matter which might bind the pebbles together makes it difficult for plants to find a solid footing, and it is challenging to find fresh water in an environment continually drenched by salt spray. It takes a very special sort of plant to cope, but nature develops ways to overcome such problems. One plant with such adaptations is the sea holly, so called because of its chosen habitat and its spiny leaves. Its bluish-green leaves are designed specifically to reduce water loss by reflecting the sun's heat, and they have a thick, waxy cuticle which protects them against the effects of sea spray. Hidden from view, the sea holly has incredibly deep roots for a plant of its size. Sometimes they reach as deep as

Top: The bar is home to several specialist plants including the sea holly, whose leaves make holly look spineless (left), and the yellow horned poppy (right).
Above: The shingle which forms the bar was pushed up by rising sea levels.

two metres, so enabling the sea holly to find water which remains less tainted by salt.

Sharing many of the sea holly's features, as well as its environment, the yellow horned poppy is another classic flower of the shingle beach, but unlike the understated, subtle blue flowers of the sea holly, the yellow horned poppy is rather brash. Its vivid yellow flowers are large and obvious, though its four petals are delicate and easily damaged by the wind. After flowering the plant develops its characteristically long and slender seed pods.

If you visit in late summer, autumn or spring, approach the lake side of the bar with caution, and scan the shore for waders – it is possible that a common, green or even wood sandpiper might be feeding there. Other waders that occasionally feed around the edge of the lake include little stint, greenshank and dunlin, whereas on the bar in winter there should be ringed plovers scampering across the pebbles. The brown, white and black plumage of these plovers creates a remarkably effective camouflage against the shingle, so look carefully. During the summer months, the many sand martins that nest in the sandy cliffs to the south of the bar will be flying over the lake and shingle in search of insects.

The return route passes Carminowe Creek and then enters woodland at Degibna, which is particularly good for fungi in autumn. The most productive areas for birds are where the woodland fringes the lake, and here it is sometimes possible to see goldcrests and firecrests among other autumnal warblers. Crossing the fields on the return to the car-park look out for bullfinches and goldfinches which are both very numerous here.

WARNING: In recent years, during the summer, the pool has suffered from algal blooms antagonized by an excess of nutrients in the water. The algae can form thick mats on the surface, robbing the water of oxygen and smothering plants on the shoreline.

Much work has been done to help improve the water quality through improvements to the treatment works in Helston, and the creation of buffer zones to prevent nitrogen run-off from surrounding fields. Do not allow dogs to drink this water.

LOOK OUT FOR

April–May: Bluebells, red campion and bugle on the verges of the track along the western shore.

May–June: Small pearl-bordered fritillary on vegetation either side of the bar.

May–August: Sand martins nest in the cliffs near Loe Bar. Sea holly, yellow-horned poppy, knapweed, wild carrot, sea campion, lady's bedstraw and sea spurge grow on the bar. A very rare species of moth, the Cornish sandhill rustic moth, is found on the bar, but is unlikely to be seen. Reed warbler, sedge warbler and reed bunting nest in the reed-beds and adjacent scrub. Great for migrant butterflies, particularly painted lady, red admiral, clouded yellow and peacock.

August–September: Look for common sandpiper and dunlin along the edge of the lake.

Winter: On the lake, tufted duck, pochard, teal, goldeneye, mallard and cormorant, along with some gadwall, pintail and shoveler, and occasional ruddy duck, scaup, and the rare ring-necked duck from North America. In recent winters there has been at least one lesser scaup; there are usually one or two great crested grebes, and occasionally a rarer grebe or diver stays for a few days after stormy weather. Water rails hide in the marshy areas but are heard more often than seen. Kingfishers may be seen along the River Cober or around the edge of the lake itself. Look out for siskin in the waterside alders near Helston.

All year: Great spotted woodpecker, nuthatch, buzzard, sparrowhawk; flocks of tits and finches. Otters live in and around the pool.

location	Walk on public rights of way
map	*Explorer* 103; *Landranger* 203
ctions to art point	By road: Take main road from Helston to the Lizard. Approx 0.5 ml before Lizard village turn R on to minor road signed Kynance Cove
ng point	SW 688 133
length	4 ml
led time	3 hours
onditions	Typical coast path, rocky and muddy in places
habitats	Coastal heath, cliff
f interest	Polurian Cove SW 668 187; Kynance Cove SW 684 133; Lizard Point lifeboat station SW 702 115
ignation	AONB, NNR, SAC
owner	NT
open	All year
entry	Charge for car-park (non-members)
enquiries	T: 01208 742 81 (NT, Lanhydrock)
facilities	

Kynance to Lizard

The Lizard peninsula epitomizes all that is beautiful about the Cornish coast. Its rugged cliffs reveal a complex geological history; its heaths and coves offer refuge for a staggering variety of wildlife, and it has a long and interesting cultural history.

The geology of the Lizard goes back some 375 million years to the Devonian period. Under the ocean, molten rock was forced, under great pressure, through the earth's crust. These igneous rocks would eventually become what we now know as the Lizard peninsula, but at that time they were completely separate from the rest of Cornwall. It was only through plate tectonics that the Lizard finally became sandwiched between Britain and Europe but, even then, there was still no English Channel. Finally, when sea levels rose after the last ice age, around 20,000 years ago, Britain became isolated from the continent by the English Channel, and the Lizard became a peninsula.

Interestingly, because geology goes some way to determining the type of vegetation that grows on the surface, the joints between the various geological features can be recognized by looking at the vegetation changes. At Polurian Cove, a few miles to the north of Kynance Cove, it is still possible to see the connection made all those years ago between Cornwall and what is now the Lizard. The geology of the Lizard is not only very complex, but also very different from the rest of Cornwall, and its flora is also quite different from the rest of the county.

The area around Kynance Cove – one of the most beautiful coves in Cornwall – offers a fine example of the type of coastal scenery of the Lizard. It is a heavily protected area, and is managed sensitively

It may look pretty, but the hottentot fig is an invasive weed at Lizard Point!

Above: Highland cattle graze the coastal heathland around Kynance.
Left: Serpentine rock was named because of its likeness to a lizard's skin.

for its archaeological and wildlife value. One strategy used here is that of conservation grazing. Old breeds of cattle, ponies and sheep are use to graze the coastal heath to help keep invasive plants at bay. Without them, gorse, bracken and blackthorn would become dominant, but through the grazing of hardy beasts such as Shetland ponies, highland cattle and Soay sheep, the scrub is kept down, and a greater diversity of habitats is created. The main benefici-

Left: Bloody cranesbill flowers in Kynance Cove.
Right: The rare thyme broomrape is a parasitic plant, taking its nutrients from the roots of wild thyme.

aries are spring flowers such as spring squill, thrift, sea campion, wild thyme and, indirectly, the parasitic plant known as thyme broomrape, but the knock-on effect is to the benefit of insects and other creatures higher up the food chain.

One feature which makes Kynance unusual is that its base rock is serpentine – a distinctive rock named because its texture is similar to a reptile's skin. A notable flower that grows here only because of the serpentine's high magnesium content is the bloody cranesbill – a species more often associated with limestone and chalk. Another species which benefits from the high magnesium content of serpentine is the Cornish heath. This species is endemic to the Lizard, but it does not flourish on all of the heath-

land of the peninsula because much of it has been covered by loess, a wind-blown sand, which prevents the roots of this heather reaching the magnesium in the underlying soil.

I suggest walking from Kynance to Lizard Point as far as the lifeboat station along the coast, and then back inland via Lizard village. Around the lifeboat station you may notice an unusual succulent growing on the cliffs: the Hottentot fig is a non-native plant introduced to Cornwall from South Africa, and though it might look attractive when in flower, it is actually smothering our natural flora. Occasionally National Trust staff abseil down the cliffs to remove as much of it as they can, but this is an arduous and time-consuming task. On a brighter note, by walking

The choughs of the Lizard are the most famous birds resident in Cornwall.

this route you should catch up with the most famous birds in Cornwall, the choughs.

When animals grazed around the whole coast of Cornwall, choughs were numerous in the county – so numerous that they even appear on our coat of arms. In the 1950s, after a downturn in grazing on marginal land brought about by the increased productivity demanded by the Second World War, the choughs died out. The connection between the chough and coastal grazing is an important one: choughs feed on beetles, grubs and larvae found on short sward,

and often show a preference for land that is grazed by livestock, particularly cattle.

After a long absence, three choughs accidentally found their way to the Lizard peninsula in 2001. Fortunately, prior to their arrival there had already been a concerted effort to revitalize the coastal heath with grazing animals, and these choughs found somewhere that they could actually live. In 2002 two of the three birds paired up and bred, making this the first breeding record of choughs in Cornwall for over 50 years.

The nest site was cloaked in secrecy, and heavily guarded around the clock by a team of volunteers against the threat posed by egg collectors, and the choughs were successful in raising three young. The following year, watched by the media and the wider public, the same pair raised another three young choughs, and their success has continued, reaching a total of 20 young raised in their first five years of breeding. Their chosen nest site, now well known, is in a small cove just to the west of Lizard Point lifeboat station, but their feeding habits often take them along the stretch of coast from the Lizard to Kynance.

The chough is similar in size to a jackdaw, but its plumage is glossy black all over, and it has a bright red bill and legs (in young birds these are pink). In flight it can be distinguished from the jackdaw by its broader wings with splayed 'finger tips', and the chough rarely flies without making a fuss. Its enthusiastic 'chi-ow' call is quite distinctive.

The name chough derives from its call, and though it is now pronounced 'chuff' it would once have been pronounced 'chow'. In fact the range of names that the chough has been given, including Cornish Daw and Cornish Jack, often reflect its voice and its distribution in England. We can be rightly proud that the only choughs breeding in England are in Cornwall.

The jackdaw is the chough's closest relative in Cornwall.

The good news continues with a second pair, made up of the original third bird and a young male from the first brood, successfully raising three young at a nest site near Porthleven in 2006. It should only be a matter of time before choughs can once again be found around the entire coast of the county.

During the breeding season, from April to June, the choughs are tightly bound to the area around Lizard Point. As the summer progresses they venture more widely, but can usually be seen along this stretch of coast. During autumn and winter some of them disperse to other parts of Cornwall, so odd birds are seen as far afield as Land's End, but the breeding pair have usually remained faithful to this general location.

LOOK OUT FOR

March–April: Spring sandwort – a flower more often associated with Arctic tundra – grows on the coast.

April–May: Green-winged orchids and early purple orchids near Kynance.

May–July: Basking sharks may be seen. Flowers of the coast include wild thyme (and thyme broomrape), thrift, sea campion, spring squill, dyer's greenweed, hairy greenweed, land quillwort, fringed rupturewort, betony, wild carrot, trefoils, wild asparagus, wild chives, harebell and 13 species of clover.

Early June: Probably the best month for watching choughs, since their young fledge about now.

Spring–Summer: Adder and common lizard.

July–September: The heath is at its most colourful, with bell heather, Cornish heath and heather. Autumn squill grows on the coast.

August–October: Lizard Point is a great place for sea-watching. Look for gannets, shearwaters, petrels, terns and skuas.

All year: Chough, peregrine, kestrel, raven and grey seal. Don't forget to look at the geology!

type of location	Nature reserve
map	*Explorer* 103; *Landranger* 203
directions to start point	By road: Take A3084 from Helston S towards Lizard Point. Approx 2 ml after turning for Mullion turn R into track signed Wild Camping; Follow track to very end, then through gate into parking area next to farm
starting point	SW 694 153
size	83 ha/205 a
recommended time	3 hours
conditions	Rough and damp under foot
habitats	Arable fields, ponds, meadow, heathland
points of interest	Windmill SW 694 152; the scrape SW 691 153; dragonfly ponds SW 691 154; Ruan Pool SW 696 158
landscape designation	AONB, LNR, SSSI
owner	Jointly owned by CWT and Cornwall Bird Watching and Preservation Society
open	All year
entry	Free
enquiries	T: 01872 273 939 (CWT)
nearest facilities	The Lizard
site facilities	

Windmill Farm

This farm-based nature reserve is unique in Cornwall. One of its remarkable features is that the whole of the farm, covering 83 hectares, is open to public access, but even more remarkable is that the arable crops, which cover around six hectares of the reserve, are never harvested. In one sense it operates as any farm would, in that crops including kale, quinoa, oats and flax, which have a marketable value, are grown; but as perverse as this might seem their seed is simply left to fall to the ground.

The aim of this strategy is to provide breeding cover and a year-round supply of food for birds – a kind of six-hectare garden bird table. Food is provided not only by the seeds of these crops, but also by the insects which find a home among their foliage. Target species such as reed bunting and linnet can find everything they need here, and their numbers have increased. Herbicides are not used on the crops, so they are interspersed with 'arable weeds' – in fact in some parts it is truer to say that the arable weeds are interspersed with crops. In winter huge flocks of common finches can be found here, along with a few less frequent species such as brambling and yellowhammer.

The vibrancy of the farm is enhanced by the varied habitats found within its border; the heathland includes both wet and dry areas. This heath is grazed by a small herd of highland cattle – a breed which can eke out sufficient nutrients in this difficult environment, while encouraging the growth of a wider range of flowers. On the drier parts, adders may be seen basking along with grayling butterflies – both are common, but equally well camouflaged as they sit motionless. Other species of butterfly found here include silver-studded blue on the dry heath;

The former windmill at Windmill Farm.

Above: The reed bunting is one species that has benefited from sympathetic management (left). Linnets, such as this female, are common at Windmill Farm (right).
Left: Goldfinches are also common on the farm.

marsh fritillary on the wetter areas, and small pearl-bordered fritillary.

Of the flowers, some of the most attractive are the orchids. Three species grow around the farm: the southern marsh orchid on damp pasture, and heath-spotted and fragrant orchids that can be seen on the heathland during June. The endemic Cornish heath blooms in profusion on the dry heath during August and September, its pink, chocolate-rimmed flowers contrasting with the bright yellow of western gorse.

The fields of grass, which for many years were cut for silage and improved by nitrogen, are now cut late in the season for hay, and in years to come meadow flowers will flourish here. These meadows are already the hunting ground for barn owls. Areas of rough grassland, combined with old airfield buildings, provide ideal conditions for this bird of prey,

This is a female black-tailed skimmer.

and what better sight to finish a day spent in the field than that of a barn owl quartering the field margins on a warm summer evening?

Soon after the reserve was purchased, scrapes and ponds were dug. Some of the ponds were deliberately surrounded by steep banks to create micro-climates of shelter and warmth specifically for dragonflies in this exposed site. Fourteen species were recorded in the first year alone, including some nationally rare breeding dragonflies such as the red-veined darter. The most unusual record was of a lesser emperor. In August the pond and surrounding banks are alive with dragonflies. The most commonly encountered are black-tailed skimmers and emperors.

Above: A female emperor dragonfly lays her eggs.
Left: A female clouded yellow butterfly.

There is a scrape specifically designed for birds at the edge of the cattle field, so the cows are responsible for keeping its margin muddy. This shallow, muddy edge is perfect for wading birds, and the best time to see them is early in the morning at periods of migration (April to May and July to September). The most frequently seen waders in late summer include the black-tailed godwit and green sandpiper, and in the winter there may be snipe, golden plover and lapwing. But because of the farm's location on Britain's most southerly tip, the list of possible waders is almost endless. It is essential that observers remain well concealed, since waders tend to be a little timid, so there is a hide overlooking the scrape, and this is the best place to sit and watch them.

Its geographical position plays an important part in dictating the species of bird, and to some extent insects, that can be seen here. During summer and early autumn, butterflies such as the red admiral, painted lady and clouded yellow can migrate here in huge numbers from the continent. Dragonflies, such as the migrant hawker, can also get caught up in this movement if suitable weather conditions (light southerly winds) prevail, but it tends to be rare birds that create most excitement.

In spring, some migratory birds that intend to fly back from Africa to the Mediterranean go too far, and find themselves accidentally on the Lizard. In this way species such as golden oriole, woodchat shrike and hoopoe can occasionally be seen on the Lizard. In the autumn we see rare pipits, larks and warblers from both east and west, blown to this headland by strong winds.

Despite many people being encouraged to the Lizard to see rare birds, it is the sad demise of farmland bird species that inspired the creation of this reserve. As a result there has been an increase in the number of common birds breeding and wintering here.

When visiting have a look in the visitor information barn.

Purple loosestrife grows in the marshy ground.

LOOK OUT FOR

April–May: An exciting time for migrating birds on the Lizard peninsula. On one day in 2003 all three native species of British harriers were seen: marsh, hen and Montagu's. Almost any bird could be encountered here.

May–June: Small pearl-bordered fritillary.

June: The marsh fritillary is probably the most significant butterfly on the reserve; others include the silver-studded blue and the grayling. Three species of orchid grow on the heathland: heath spotted, southern marsh and fragrant.

June–September: Dragonflies present in good numbers. Look out for the red-veined darter, black-tailed skimmer and emperor. Barn owls may be seen hunting over the rough grassland in the evenings.

July–September: Green sandpiper and black-tailed godwit are two waders which visit the scrapes. The endemic Cornish heath is found here in great quantities; purple loosestrife grows in the damp patches.

Winter: Large flocks of lapwing and golden plover use the field near Ruan Pool; flocks of finches and buntings take advantage of the seed in the arable fields. The commonest birds in these flocks are chaffinch, linnet, goldfinch, skylark, reed bunting and greenfinch; less frequent species, such as brambling and yellowhammer, may also be attracted.

Nature reserve

Explorer 103; *Landranger* 203, 204

By road: From Helston take A3083 S towards the Lizard; turn L at roundabout after RNAS Culdrose on to B3293. Immediately after Earth Station, car-park on R signed National Nature Reserve

SW 729 212

120 ha/300 a

Described walk is 6 ml (for wheelchair users, a 400-metre path)

3 hours

Difficult, uneven clumps of grass, often wet underfoot

Heath, coniferous woodland, pools

From car-park use map references to assist in finding route: SW 707 195; SW 723 184; SW 729194. Standing stone at SW 726 213

AONB, NNR, SAC, SSSI

NE

All year

Free

T: 01872 265 710 (NE, Truro)

St Keverne

Goonhilly Downs

The vast, level plain that forms Goonhilly Downs is interrupted only by occasional stunted pine trees, lichen-covered posts, and unusually large mounds of heather. The horizon is distant, and the sky large.

Our influence on the Downs is all around, since we are responsible for the formation of the entire area. Once this heath would have been a woodland, but our ancestors, keen to develop an area in which to graze their animals, performed the sort of 'slash and burn' for which other nations now receive our disapproval. Scattered across the heath are a number of Bronze Age burial mounds, and close to the Goonhilly Earth Station there is a standing stone. The Earth Station is the biggest of its kind in the world, and has dominated the skyline of Goonhilly since it was built in 1962. Its largest dish stands some 46 metres high. The most recent addition to the surrounding area is the wind farm at Bonython Manor.

The atmosphere of Goonhilly changes not only with the seasons, but also with the time of day and state of the weather, so all of these factors must be considered when planning a visit. Early in the morning on a calm summer's day, when the mist finds damp hollows over which to form, there is a definite magic to this heath. Each and every web, formed by a myriad spiders, is bedecked with dew and highlighted by the light of the rising sun. Gradually the sun burns back the mist, creating a heat that brings life to the many insects and reptiles of the heath, until it once more falls in the sky to the west. Dusk brings with it a whole new atmosphere, and it is then that the sounds of the heath become a more significant feature, when the eerie churring of a nightjar combines with the songs of grasshoppers

Bell heather grows in the shadow of the Earth Station.

An early morning mist on Goonhilly.

and crickets, as well as the distant reeling of grass-hopper warblers.

Probably the most important type of natural history present on site is the flora. The heath is renowned for its heathers, and here there are four types: heather; bell heather; cross-leaved heath and Cornish heath. Heather, often known as ling, has small, pale pink flowers which rely upon each other for their effect. The flowers of bell heather are of a much deeper pink, and being larger, and bell-shaped, they are more obvious. Cross-leaved heath is extremely widespread at Goonhilly, but nowhere does it grow in the high density of the other heathers. Its individual flowers are pale pink, and though they have the same shape as those of bell heather they grow in characteristic small clusters at the top of the stem. The last of the heathers, the Cornish heath, is the most significant since it is endemic to the Lizard peninsula. Its flower spikes are the most impressive of all the heathers, with a mass of quite large and often colourful flowers. Individual colours vary from white to deep pink, but each tiny flower has an attractive, red-brown rim. To

Above: The early morning dew creates jewels on the spiders' webs.
Right: Adders bask among heather on heathland.

encourage the flowers, a herd of ponies grazes here from June to September.

One of the best sections of the heath, in terms of its diversity of flora, has been made accessible to all, with a level-surfaced footpath adjacent to a car-park. Here all of the heathers can be seen growing in the shadow of the Earth Station. Longer walks are possible, and for those who come prepared with boots and weather-proof clothes I recommend a circular

Left: Bog asphodel is very common on Goonhilly. Right: The great burnet can be found on the heath.

route along the bridleway towards Penhale, turning left along the perimeter fence, and left again along a permissive path towards Croft Pascoe 'forest'. After skirting the easterly edge of Croft Pascoe, head back to the car-park, using the Earth Station as a guide.

Over most of the heath the dominant species are not heathers but bog-rush and purple moor grass. The bog asphodel is surprisingly numerous, even when long, hot summers create extremely dry conditions, and the dark, wine-red flowers of great burnet are scattered across the heath in mid-summer. Perhaps the most beautiful flowers on the grassy areas of the

heath bloom during June. They are two very special species of orchid: the heath spotted and the fragrant.

When damper conditions hang on into summer, the heath has many small pools which come to life with dragonflies. The drier areas play host to butter-flies, with just a few specialist species living and breeding here. Of these, the grayling is probably the most obvious, despite its wonderful camouflage. At night, the heath is alive with moths. One of the biggest is the emperor moth, whose wings are adorned with huge eye-spots, to make it look threatening to would-be predators. Though we are unlikely to see one of these moths during the day, it is worth looking out for their colourful green- and pink-spotted caterpillars. There are also moths flying by day on the heath, and this is a great location for seeing some of our migrant species, such as the silver-Y moth and the hummingbird hawkmoth, particularly when calm conditions prevail.

The range of birds is slightly limited by the lack of variety in habitat types, but those that can be found here are often very special. The most exciting encounters are likely in autumn and winter, when raptors (birds of prey) can sometimes be seen. The merlin is a fast-flying, but incredibly small falcon, which can be seen in the area mostly during autumn. Hen harriers and short-eared owls often occur here during the winter, while it is possible to see kestrels, buzzards and barn owls throughout the year. Patches of water are always worth a closer look. In late summer a muddy margin to a small pool might play host to a green or wood sandpiper, whereas in winter it is more likely to be a snipe or a woodcock.

Cornish heath is endemic to the Lizard.

LOOK OUT FOR

March–September: Reptiles – common lizard and adder.

May–June: Cuckoo.

June: Heath spotted and fragrant orchids.

June–July: Bog asphodel, round-leaved sundew, sawwort, black knapweed, great burnet, wood sage, betony, dropwort, lady's bedstraw, wild thyme and tormentil.

Summer: Butterflies including grayling, silver-studded blue, small skipper and small heath; moths, including the resident emperor as well as many migrants such as the silver-Y and hummingbird hawkmoth; many species of dragonfly are present; breeding birds including nightjar and grasshopper warbler.

July–September: Heather, bell heather, cross-leaved heath, and Cornish heath are all in flower on the dry heath; purple loosestrife, meadowsweet and royal fern around the damp areas; green and wood sandpipers may stop off at the pools to feed.

November–February: Short-eared owl, merlin, hen harrier, woodcock and snipe.

All year: Purple moor grass and bog-rush; stonechat, meadow pipit, skylark, raven, buzzard, kestrel, barn owl, linnet, long-tailed tit and goldcrest; fox. Croft Pascoe forest holds the most westerly British record of the rare but rather colourful yellow and black spider, whose scientific name is *Argiope bruennichi*.

site number	# 25
type of location	Nature reserve
map	*Explorer* 104; *Landranger* 204
directions to start point	By road: Take A393 from Redruth towards Falmouth; on entering Ponsanooth go over bridge, turn immediately R: narrow road leads through housing area and up a hill. Park sensibly in village; continue up hill on foot. Entrance to reserve just outside village, along footpath to R
starting point	SW 754 376
size	8 ha/20 a
length	Circular walk approx 1.5 ml
recommended time	2 hours
conditions	Part good, on track; part very uneven and wet, on rocky footpath
habitats	Woodland and fast-flowing river
points of interest	Mills and bridge over river SW 748 373; northerly extent of circular walk SW 753 376
landscape designation	LNR
owner	CWT
open	All year
entry	Free
enquiries	T: 01872 273 939 (CWT)
nearest facilities	Ponsanooth
site facilities	

Kennall Vale

When, in 1985, the Cornwall Wildlife Trust took on the lease of the beautifully wooded valley of Kennall Vale near Ponsanooth, they took on much more than just a wildlife sanctuary, for deep in the woods of Kennall Vale lies the best-preserved gunpowder works in the south-west of Britain.

There is some speculation that gunpowder may have been manufactured in Cornwall as early as the eighteenth century, but references to it are not clear enough to be certain. What is clear is that the flourishing mining industry had developed an appetite for the use of gunpowder since it was first used to blast rocks in the early seventeenth century. There was obviously great economic potential for the first local manufacturers of this compound, and it was only a matter of time until it was made in the county. All the early activity centred on Ponsanooth when, in 1809, a gunpowder mill was set up at Cosawes Wood by Nicholls & Gill. The Fox family, who began building a much larger processing works in Kennall Vale after being granted a licence in 1811, soon took over the Cosawes plant.

The two important factors regarding the positioning of a gunpowder works at Kennall Vale were the availability of running water to drive the machinery, and the dense cover provided by woodland to inhibit the effects of any accidental explosions. The mill buildings in the vale were in advance of any others in that they were of very solid construction. Built of cut granite blocks, their walls were intended to withstand explosions, whereas their large windows, which overlooked the river, and light roofs were intended to act as 'blow-out' protection.

In 1844 expansion of the works led to the construction of new buildings on the south side of the valley

The valley is alive with the sound of crashing water.

Left: Ruined buildings and old leats create a unique atmosphere in Kennall Vale.
Above: Ivy grows on every wall and nearly every tree.

in Roches Wood. The Roches section offered a new and complete processing works incorporating all the latest techniques, but the old works were used continually until the demise of the entire factory. At its peak during the 1860s the works employed over 50 people, but by the 1880s it was becoming apparent that the production of gunpowder in Cornwall was soon to become uneconomical. The Kennall Vale company had already seen the writing on the wall when it established the dynamite factory at Upton Towans. It sold the Kennall Vale factory in 1898, to a national gunpowder company, Curtis's & Harvey, who were still buying out all of the competition, for the then princely sum of £25,826 17 shillings and 6 pence.

Top: Dippers can be seen along the river in Kennall Vale.
Above: Grey wagtails often nest in the old buildings.

Look out for the scarlet elf cup fungus if visiting in February.

The Kennall Vale site was subsequently used for a variety of minor purposes, but the buildings were eventually sold off, some as late as the 1950s. During the twentieth century, little changed, so many of the buildings can still be seen today. On entering the reserve, the first buildings around the quarry are of the newer development (1844) known as Roches Section. Some of the buildings here were lost when the quarry was excavated, and many are being reclaimed by nature with trees growing through the walls, while mosses, lichens and ferns grow on them. Here the woodland is tranquil and quiet; the steep valley sides protect the trees from any wind, and the pool in the quarry lies motionless.

Further down into the valley the sound of crashing water among the rock-strewn riverbed is dominant. The spray from the falls adds to the cool, misty atmosphere in the depths of the valley. The various leats and waterwheel pits provide water, and surfaces on which lichens and mosses can thrive. Where once there was great human activity, ivy now clings to buildings, enhancing the sense of desertion.

This environment is perfect for two birds which specialize in fast-flowing rivers: the dipper and the grey wagtail. The dipper is a bird about the size and colour of a blackbird, but with a white breast and subtle, chocolate-brown belly. It lives along river courses, finding its food under the water's surface, and its skill in doing so is quite breathtaking. Even in the fastest of rapids the dipper can walk into the water, using its understanding of hydrodynamics to remain in contact with the river bed. This incredibly

Wood anemones are just one of the many spring flowers which add interest to Kennall Vale.

of habitat should leave no confusion. Grey wagtails eat insects at the edge of the water, but sometimes make aerial sallies in pursuit of their prey. They have plenty of choices for nest sites in Kennall Vale, since they like to nest in walls clad with ivy and moss.

In spring, before the trees develop their full foliage, the woodland is a beautiful scene with many wood anemones and bluebells. The combination of humidity and old, decaying wood provides ideal conditions for fungi, many of which are present only in autumn, but one to look out for here is the scarlet elf cup, which peaks in February.

To explore the reserve, follow the footpath from the road straight down to the river. From here there are footpaths along both sides of the river. Start by walking downstream on one bank, and return on the other. My experiences at Kennall Vale have always been positive ones: stepping into the valley is like stepping into another world.

buoyant bird occasionally bobs to the surface, like a cork, with an unfortunate larva or insect, before swimming to the bottom again in search of more. The dipper builds a dome-shaped nest under the roots of trees at the side of the river or, occasionally, in structures such as bridges or old mills. The name 'dipper' comes from the bird's habit of continual bobbing – a strategy which may seem foolish, but which often helps it to blend with the fast-moving water and reflections of its surroundings.

Even more enthusiastically, grey wagtails wag their tails with fervour, as if to communicate visually in this noisy environment. Their bright yellow under parts lead many people to mis-identify them as yellow wagtails, but their grey backs and choice

---

LOOK OUT FOR

February: The scarlet elf cup – a small, red fungus.

April–May: The valley is at its most beautiful, with plenty of woodland flowers including wood anemone, wood sorrel and bluebells.

Summer: Breeding birds such as the spotted flycatcher, dipper and grey wagtail. Flowers, including sanicle and yellow pimpernel. The speckled wood butterfly is common; the most appealing butterfly is the silver-washed fritillary.

Autumn: Good for fungi.

All year: Great spotted woodpecker and nuthatch are resident. The valley is incredibly green, with plenty of ivy, and a wonderful range of mosses, lichens and ferns growing on the ground, in the trees and on the old buildings. The most significant fern here is the Tunbridge filmy fern, which grows on damp surfaces.

e of location	Nature reserve and walk
map	*Explorer* 104; *Landranger* 204
directions to start point	By road: From A39 Truro to Falmouth road turn R at foot of hill near Devoran, signed to Bissoe. 0.25 ml past Bissoe turn R into car-park by cycle hire centre
tarting point	SW 769 415
size	3 ha/7.5 a
length	7 ml (to Devoran and back)
ended time	3 hours
conditions	Good footpaths with gravel surface
habitats	Pools, river, scrub, estuary
ts of interest	Nature reserve at SW 771 413; creek-side at Devoran SW 799 388
designation	AONB (part), LNR
owner	CWT
open	Privately owned car-park open 9.30 am to 5.30 pm daily (closes 4.30 pm in winter)
entry	Charge for parking
enquiries	T: 01872 273 939 (CWT)
site facilities	

Bissoe Valley

The story of the Bissoe Valley is one of absolute exploitation. Throughout our history we have been responsible for taking anything and everything that might be of value from our surroundings, without a thought for the health of the environment, or the possible consequences for ourselves.

If we look back in time to the seventeenth century and earlier, the village of Bissoe was a port situated on a navigable river, but through the combined processes of mining and tin-streaming the river became silted, and the whole valley bottom was filled with mining waste. When the Wheal Jane mine was first opened in the eighteenth century, its main target was pyrite, which was used in the making of sulphuric acid. Mining continued until recent times when the now infamous 'new' Wheal Jane mine was opened in the 1970s to exploit the tin ore found in the valley. This mine was never easy to operate, and although it processed 300,000 tons of ore each year it needed to pump out a staggering three million gallons of water every day. In 1991 this mine closed, and when the pumps were turned off in January 1992 tens of millions of gallons of heavily polluted, acidic water escaped into the valley.

This was a turning point in the history of the valley, and since then people have started to value the positive aspects of this landscape. One major development has been the formation of the Mineral Tramways network of footpaths and cycle ways. The Bissoe Valley lies at the heart of the Coast to Coast cycle route which links the nearby creekside village of Devoran with the popular north coast village of Portreath – a total distance of around 12 miles (19 km).

Water lilies and fringed water lilies grow on a pool at Bissoe.

Above: The keeled skimmer enjoys the acidic nature of this reserve.
Left: The scarce blue-tailed damselfly occurs at only a handful of locations in Cornwall.

Though much of the Bissoe Valley is blighted by the effects of mining, its bare ground laced with heavy metals that resist the growth of plants, there are positive aspects, and one of those is the Cornwall Wildlife Trust reserve situated close to the village of Bissoe. The four areas of wetland, combined with the nearby River Carnon, create a natural oasis of calm and beauty. The small, rush- and reed-fringed lakes each have their own character, and varying levels of water. In summer the surface of one is smothered with water lilies. There is the common white water lily, which is probably hybridized with cultivated varieties, but the more spectacular variety here is the fringed water lily, its vivid yellow flower creating a splendid backdrop to the activity that continues throughout the summer at these pools.

From June to September the edges of the water are bristling with dragonflies, and this has to be one

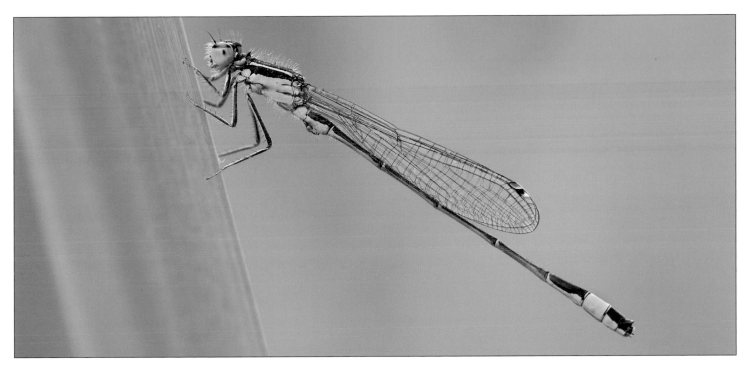

Top: Blue-tailed damselfly is one of our commonest species.
Above: The emerald damselfly is distinctive because it holds its wings only half closed.

Swallows hunt for insects over the water.

of the most easily accessible places in the county to see them. Seventeen species occur here regularly. The most exciting to the specialist are probably the scarce blue-tailed damselflies, and maybe the keeled skimmers, but to the casual observer the large dragon-flies such as the emperors and hawkers are the most impressive, while the wonderful colours of the smaller damselflies are also memorable.

The smaller damselflies are easier to watch at the drier parts of the reserve. They perch on vegetation and allow a fairly close approach. The larger species are much more mobile, and their identification is usually easiest with binoculars. At first the mass of movement and colour can be confusing, but as with any form of wildlife-watching it is just a matter of 'getting your eye in'. Armed with a good field guide, learn to identify one or two species while they are at rest, and then watch how they behave. In time, you will even be able to identify some of them in flight.

It is fascinating to watch as swallows skim the surface of the ponds to collect a mouthful of water to drink. Occasionally they seem to dip a little too far, but such is their mastery of the air that this apparent miscalculation actually allows them to take a splash-bath. Running over the lily pads may be a young moorhen chasing its mother back into the shelter of the rushes. An occasional croak from the shallow pond edges indicates the presence of a common toad or common frog, and Cornwall's only species of newt, the palmate newt, also lives here.

Common toads spawn in the ponds at Bissoe.

Among the soft rushes and reeds there are also bulrushes, southern marsh orchids, and flag iris, but the wider valley has a limited variety of plant life, being dominated by gorse and heather. One species that does grow well here is the common centaury – a pretty pink flower; teasels abound further down the valley, and a buddleia is never far away. Birds in the valley include bullfinch, greenfinch, goldfinch, linnet and long-tailed tit, while kestrel, sparrowhawk and buzzard may be seen soaring overhead.

The nature reserve is found by following the cycleway from the car-park in the direction of Devoran. To enhance a visit to the area I suggest continuing the walk from here down to the creek at Devoran. Along the way you will pass the Wheal Jane Pilot Passive Treatment Plant – two series of reed-beds designed to purify floodwater from the mine. If you choose to walk as far as Devoran, then a good place for lunch is on the quayside overlooking Restronguet Creek: here a whole new habitat opens out, offering the chance of seeing a good variety of waders. The optimum months for seeing waders are from August to March, so to link this with a trip to see dragonflies I suggest a visit during late August. Arriving at Devoran a couple of hours before high tide should provide the opportunity to see redshank, greenshank, curlew, black-tailed godwit and dunlin.

LOOK OUT FOR

This site is mentioned mostly for dragonflies. These are the species you might see, and approximate flight periods:

Beautiful demoiselle: May–August

Emerald damselfly: June–September

Azure damselfly: May–August

Common blue damselfly: May–September

Blue-tailed damselfly: May–September

Scarce blue-tailed damselfly: June–September

Large red damselfly: April–September

Southern hawker: July–September

Common hawker: July–September

Migrant hawker: August–October

Emperor dragonfly: June–August

Golden-ringed dragonfly: June–August

Broad-bodied chaser: May–July

Four-spotted chaser: June–August

Black-tailed skimmer: May–July

Keeled skimmer: June–August

Common darter: June–October

Others:

August–March: Waders on the creek include dunlin, curlew, oystercatcher, greenshank and black-tailed godwit.

January–March: Best time for amphibians, with common frog, common toad and palmate newt spawning. Gorse in flower.

May–June: Southern marsh orchid, flag iris and broom.

July–September: Purple loosestrife, agrimony, common centaury, buddleia and heather in flower.

type of location	Walk on public rights of way
map	*Explorer* 105; *Landranger* 204
directions to start point	By road: From Truro take A390 towards St Austell. On entering Tresillian village park in lay-by on R
starting point	SW 860 456
length	St Clement and return: 2.5 ml; Malpas and return: 4 ml
recommended time	St Clement: 1.5 hours; Malpas: 2.5 hours
conditions	Level, easy walking, sometimes muddy
habitats	Woodland, creek, pond
points of interest	Tresemple Pond SW 855 446; St Clement (limited parking available) SW 852 438; Malpas SW 845 427
landscape designation	AONB, SAC
site facilities	*Note:* Park at St Clement for limited wheelchair access. Refreshments in Malpas.

Tresillian River

Most of the Fal estuary complex is excellent for bird-watching, but some spots are consistently more productive than others. Even so, places that are teeming with birds at one time of day might be devoid of life at another. Times of the day, month of the year, and states of tide are all just as critical as the location for a worthwhile visit. My own favourite bit of the whole estuary for bird-watching is a small stretch of footpath between St Clement and Tresillian.

This walk is a linear one, from Tresillian to St Clement and back, or it can be extended to Malpas for interest or refreshments. The path follows the edge of the river where, at low tide, there is a large area of mud for wading birds to probe for food and, at high tide, the same birds are forced to congregate in predictable places above the high-water level. Importantly, there is one such area that can be seen well from this path, at Tresemple Pond.

It is essential that before planning a visit you consider the time of year and the time of the tide. June and July are not productive times for seeing wading birds on estuaries in Cornwall. During August birds start to return from their breeding grounds, and through September and October we see a good variety of species which may include some less common ones. November to March sees the highest number of birds, but with slightly less potential for rarer types. In April and May we see a return of the passage birds, but a gradual decline in the total number present.

State of tide is critical at any estuary location. At low tide birds can be distant, though along this footpath the problem is not so much one of distance as that birds disappear down a channel in the creek. At high tide birds are forced off the mud on to high-tide

The hamlet of St Clement sits on the Tresillian River.

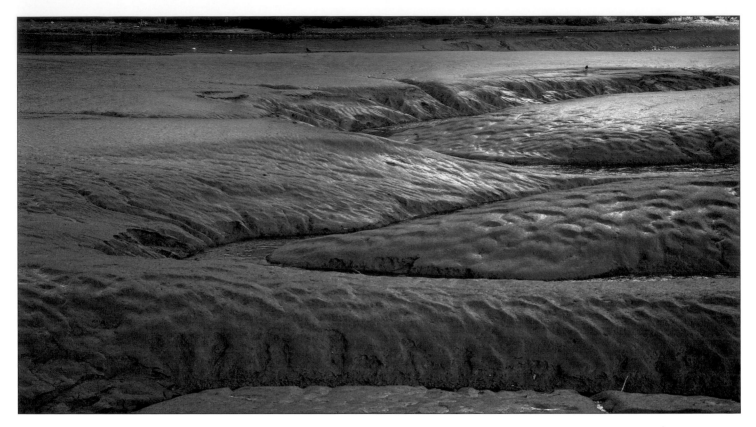

The muddy creek at low tide.

roosts, which can be useful if you know where they are, but not much good if you don't. Usually the best time to visit an estuary is on a rising tide, a couple of hours before high tide, when birds are gradually forced nearer to the edges of the creek, where we can get our best views.

At the Tresillian end of this footpath is an area of wetland and reeds, which are good for breeding reed and sedge warblers in summer, and provide a temporary home to water rails in winter. From here the path towards St Clement is frequently masked from the river by mature oak trees, making wading birds less wary of our presence, and so providing the opportunity for closer views. In winter the most obvious bird is the curlew, which is easily identi-

fied by its long, down-curved bill. Another simple one to identify is the shelduck, which breeds and overwinters on the creek. This is a large duck with colourful green and brown patterns on a white body. Redshank, dunlin, greenshank, grey heron and little egret are also numerous and obvious here.

There are other species at this site which are a little less well known. Another large wader frequently seen here is the black-tailed godwit. This is far more common in winter than in summer, so you won't see the brick-red breeding plumage that the field guides often show. The long, straight bill, which sometimes looks slightly up-curved, is indicative of a godwit. To distinguish the black-tailed from the bar-tailed godwit, look for the white bottom, black and white

Above: The legs of a redshank in winter vary between brown and red (left). The greenshank has a slightly upturned bill (right).
Left: A spotted redshank in winter plumage.

wing pattern and, of course, the black tail; the bar-tailed godwit has plain brown wings and barring on the tail.

The most unusual wading bird found here between September and March is the spotted redshank. Before we can identify one with confidence, it is important to consider two commoner species – the redshank and the greenshank. The redshank is a medium-sized wader, much smaller than the curlew but larger than a dunlin. It has red legs and a straight, medium-length, red bill. The redshank is basically a brown bird, but in flight it has a white trailing edge to its wing as well as a white rump and tail. The greenshank is chunkier than the redshank, and in winter it

Above: Reeds are found along the riverside.
Left: Little grebe, in summer plumage.

has a white belly and grey back. Its bill and legs are grey-green, and in flight it has a white rump and tail, but lacks any white on the wings.

The spotted redshank is almost like a cross between the two. It has red legs and a red bill like the redshank, but its bill is longer and finer. Its overall size is more like that of a greenshank, and like the greenshank it is very pale underneath in winter (though its plumage is darker in spring and early autumn). In flight the spotted redshank lacks the white wing bar

Water rails are secretive birds, found here in winter.

Tresemple Pond. Take care if you are the first person to walk across the footpath between creek and pool, because you may disturb birds resting there. Pause adjacent to bushes so that your outline is less obvious, and use binoculars to identify the birds.

On the pond in winter will be a good number of little grebes. These tiny birds are easily overlooked, since they are continually diving for small fish and underwater insects. When disturbed they dive, rather than flying away, and can stay under water for a surprisingly long period, covering a great distance. In winter at the reedy edge of the pool close to the path there are sometimes snipe and water rail. Both of these species are very secretive and usually difficult to see. It is not unusual to see kingfishers in winter: listen for their thin, whistling call.

of the redshank, making it look a little like a greenshank with a red bill! In terms of behaviour it is more common to see a spotted redshank swimming than either the redshank or greenshank.

At high tide it is sometimes possible to see all three of these species side by side at the far end of

---

LOOK OUT FOR

April–May: Sometimes possible to see whimbrel along this stretch of river; breeding migrants return, including reed and sedge warblers near Tresillian.

Summer: Shelduck breed in adjacent woodland, bringing their young out on to the mud to feed; buzzard and sparrowhawk also breed in surrounding woodland; glasswort on marshes.

September–October: Wading birds: it is usually possible to see redshank, spotted redshank, greenshank, curlew, black-tailed godwit and dunlin; other species sometimes present include green sandpiper, common sandpiper and bar-tailed godwit.

Winter: Kingfishers are possible anywhere – the best place to look for them is at the pond. The same pond often holds a variety of ducks and grebes; as well as the regular mallard, teal, shelduck and little grebes, there are occasionally wigeon, tufted duck, pochard and goldeneye. Water rail and snipe inhabit the reedy margins of the pool. The creek is good for waders throughout winter.

location Garden

map *Explorer* 105; *Landranger* 204

directions to start point By road: Take B3273 S from St Austell towards Mevagissey; turn R at Tregiskey, signed to The Lost Gardens of Heligan

start point SW 997 468

size 81 ha/200 a

length Open

suggested time Day

conditions Good footpaths

habitats Formal garden, lakes, woodland, meadow, scrub, farmland

other interest Lakes in Lost Valley SX 003 463; Horsemoor SX 002 467

owner The Lost Gardens of Heligan

open All year except Christmas Day, Christmas Eve, 10 am to 5 pm

entry Charge

enquiries T: 01726 845 100 (LGH)

facilities *Note:* Dogs on leads October–June; no dogs July–September

The Lost Gardens of Heligan

Formal gardens are not always the best places to go to see wildlife, but many are now claiming green credentials by creating conservation areas, suitable for our native species. Some, I suspect, are simply jumping on the bandwagon of public opinion and paying lip service to what could be a very important role. Heligan, however, is doing very much more than that.

It is difficult, when visiting Heligan for the first time, to avoid feeling a little daunted by the size of the gardens. The 81 hectares are split into many different compartments, with numerous entrances and exits between them. It is quite easy to get lost here, even with leaflets and signs to help, but we can only imagine the excitement and anticipation that must have captured the minds of Tim Smit and John Willis back in 1990 when they began to rediscover the then truly 'lost' gardens of Heligan.

In the century and a half leading up to the First World War the garden was a thriving environment, but with most of its staff called up for active service, and many of them failing to return home, the gardens began to fall into disrepair. Many secrets of the gardens' make-up and management were concealed by years of neglect, but slowly these secrets are being rediscovered and again put into practice. It could be argued that this neglect is likely to have been good for our natural history, and that the re-development of the garden may have been detrimental to it, but it has always been the aim of the management of Heligan to provide an environment in which wildlife can thrive.

There is always colour in the gardens at Heligan.

Above: Barn owls nest in specially erected nest boxes, and can be seen on camera.
Left: Horsemoor Hide has plenty of interactive media for children to enjoy.

For wildlife enthusiasts, a visit to Heligan must begin with the wildlife project, and the first stop-off point has to be the wildlife hide at Horsemoor, which is lavish and impressive. This isn't the sort of facility found in a typical nature reserve. I couldn't help but feel a little sorry for less prosperous wildlife organizations, like the Wildlife Trust, when I played with the rotating CCTV camera and flicked between live action from the barn owl nest box and recorded activity of the badger sett from the night before.

Above: Badgers can be watched by CCTV, or on special evenings.
Right: Pipistrelle bats roost at Heligan, and can be watched on CCTV.

The entertaining video footage showed badger cubs emerging from their sett, playing with each other and foraging with their mother. It seemed like nothing wild could move without being covered by at least one of the cameras. Some creatures, such as the pipistrelle bats in the Steward's House, didn't move very much, but it was fascinating to listen to their squeaks and twitters through the audio system. This really is a great place for all the family, so if you want to involve children in wildlife look no further.

Common birds such as the chaffinch flock to the picnic tables in search of scraps.

Even though most of the images are live, it is easy to become detached from the wildlife when it is viewed through electronic media. But we must not forget that staff at Heligan have done a lot of work to encourage the wild animals to use their land. Nest boxes have been erected; a wild garden has been planted; meadows are cut late in the summer to encourage the growth of wild flowers; trees are being planted, and hedgerows are being cared for through traditional laying techniques. By way of a 'thank you', a pair of barn owls immediately took up residence in the very first nest box erected, and they have successfully raised young under the spotlight of the CCTV system. The barn owls, together with other animals, now thrive in an increasingly healthy ecosystem.

Outside the hide hangs a wide range of bird food, attracting an equally wide range of birds, from nuthatch to goldfinch, and blue tit to great spotted woodpecker. Inside the hide, samples of bird foods are provided, along with a challenge to match the food to the bird species that eats it. The pond, which has been specially created in front of the hide, is home to dragonflies, damselflies, newts, frogs and toads, but is also used by birds to drink and bathe. All this action is played out within easy watching distance of the hide, and binoculars are provided for a closer look.

Before trying the outdoor nature trails it is wise to partake of light refreshments on the Steward's Meadow, where a plethora of garden birds will help clean up the crumbs. Blackbirds, song thrushes, house sparrows, robins, dunnocks … the list goes on

A honey bee makes the most of Heligan's hospitality.

Don't overlook the more formal gardens. Apart from being attractive to us, they also attract wildlife. I can well remember seeing a pair of goldcrests feeding in the bamboo at the foot of the Jungle, and even a firecrest there one autumn. Late summer is a good time for seeing the rather bizarre-looking hummingbird hawkmoth, which flies by day and hovers while drinking nectar from flowers.

There is nowhere else in Cornwall quite like Heligan. The fact that visitors are guaranteed to see CCTV footage of wild animals means that everyone, from young to old, should have an exciting wildlife experience here, and that must be worth more than any words or photos in a book.

... all have become accustomed to the presence of a large number of human cake-eaters!

Notices along the nature trails inform visitors about what can be seen – not just the actual wildlife, but also the tracks and signs, such as the trails left by visiting badgers. Also of interest are the details given about the plants that can be seen around the estate, including their medicinal uses. For example, did you know that the common reed was once used to treat cholera? The notices at Heligan are all relevant, and will enrich your experience of the wildlife here.

The trails lead visitors into the Lost Valley, with its river and lakes. Here wild creatures escape the 'big brother' cameras, and it is down to the observer to observe. Bluebells grow in the woods, and around the lakes grow flag iris and marsh marigold. Kingfishers can be seen here throughout the year, though the vegetation is dense in summer, making them difficult to spot. Over the lake on warm summer days a mass of small insects hovers like a cloud, but thankfully spotted flycatchers can be seen doing their best to catch them all! Other resident birds around the lakes include grey wagtail and the ubiquitous mallard.

LOOK OUT FOR

April–May: Early spring flowers typical of woodland include primrose, lesser celandine, wood anemone and bluebell. Birds' nest-building is watched by CCTV.

May–June: Around the lakes cuckoo flower and flag iris bloom.

May–August: One of the stars of the show is the pair of barn owls using a purpose-built nest box. Badgers become more active as the cubs explore their territories: either watch CCTV footage or attend a special evening event. Summer migrants include spotted flycatcher, blackcap, garden warbler and chiffchaff in the woods. Good for dragonflies around the lakes in the Lost Valley and near Horsemoor hide. Swallows nest in the farm buildings; the formal gardens are alive with insects: look for bees, butterflies and hummingbird hawkmoths.

Autumn: Good for fungi: look out for stump puffballs and fly agaric.

Winter–early Spring: Great activity among common birds around the bird-feeding station.

All year: Great spotted woodpecker, green woodpecker, treecreeper, nuthatch, goldcrest and mistle thrush.

Luxulyan Valley

location Walk on public rights of way

map *Explorer* 107; *Landranger* 200

tions to By road: From Luxulyan take minor
rt point road towards Lanlivery; outside
village take first R; after about 0.5
ml car-park on L just before viaduct

g point SX 058 573

length 3 ml (return to Ponts Mill);
or 5 ml (return to St Blazey)

ed time 2 or 3 hours

nditions Track and path, some uneven
and wet surfaces

habitats Woodland, river, marsh

interest Treffry Viaduct SX 056 572;
Ponts Mill SX 073 562

gnation AGLV

open All year

entry Free

acilities Luxulyan

acilities

The Luxulyan Valley is heavily wooded, and has plenty of natural interest. Such habitat is not common in wind-blown Cornwall, but what also sets this valley apart from others of its kind is the influence of our own hand. Our manipulation of the environment has been considerable, but the processes of nature have utilized and softened our work to produce something unique.

Parking by the Treffry Viaduct it is impossible not to be struck by the scale of this structure. The viaduct stands at about 100 feet high and 650 feet long, its ten arches each span 40 feet, and it is estimated that 200,000 cubic feet of granite was used to build it. It is astonishing to think that the whole viaduct – the first of stone construction in Cornwall – was built in only three years (1839–42). Its purposes were two-fold: to carry both a tramway and a leat across the valley. Its overall aim, like that of all the other structures along the valley, was to transport rocks and minerals – granite, tin or copper – from the Luxulyan Valley down to the port at Par.

The viaduct is, in fact, an aqueduct, and if you walk across the top it is still possible to see water running beneath the surface layer of granite slabs. The mechanisms for moving rock and ore down to Par included horse-drawn tramways, water-powered inclined tramways, and canals. To provide sufficient water, it was decided that the viaduct would need to transport water from the other side of the valley, and a series of leats was created to serve the system further down the line. The whole scheme is an amazing feat of ingenuity, engineering, and perseverance.

A variety of walks are possible, though I think the best strategy for a visit is to walk from the Treffry Viaduct, staying on the north side of the river, to

The path into the wood meanders alongside a leat.

Ponts Mill or possibly St Blazey. Throughout this stretch you will see evidence of inclined tramways, canals, leats, waterwheel pits, and so on, and there are some interpretation panels. Returning along the same side of the river, along the same or an alternative pathway, is probably the best option.

One of the best places to observe the river is near the car-park. Here, among the boulders in the river, it is worth looking for dipper and grey wagtail. The clearing formed by the small road is a good spot for butterflies such as orange tip and brimstone in spring, followed by speckled wood and silver-washed fritillary in summer. The mature beech trees on the path to the top of the viaduct have plenty of nest holes, and it should be possible to see nuthatch and great-spotted woodpecker here.

The nuthatch is a surprisingly small bird, not much bigger than a tit. It spends most of its time running around on the trunks and branches of trees looking for grubs and insects. Unlike the woodpeckers, with which it invites comparison, the nuthatch can run up or down a vertical tree trunk. It makes its home in a tree hole, and will readily take to nest boxes, but is often quite fussy about the entranceway to its nest: it must be the right size. If a nuthatch finds a suitable spot but the doorway is too big, it will plaster mud around the hole to make it smaller.

From the viaduct there is a great view over the valley, so have a look for birds of prey, particularly on days when the sun creates thermals on which they can soar. Sparrowhawks and buzzards are the most common. Being able to look into the tree canopy from a height might put you eye to eye with birds such as willow warblers, blackcap and bullfinch. Also flying from one side of the valley to the other you may see a jay: this is a particularly busy bird in autumn, when it flies back and forth collecting acorns to bury in the leaf litter of its territory. Listen for its loud and

The Treffry Viaduct is also an aqueduct.

Top: The marsh tit has a sooty black cap.
Above: Long-tailed tits frequent Luxulyan Valley.

Above: Jays spend their autumn collecting acorns.
Left: Nuthatches have the ability to run up and down tree trunks.

coarse shrieks, which are often the first sign of the jay's presence.

To walk through the woodland along the valley towards Ponts Mill is a wonderful experience. Crashing water from leats and streams creates a perfect environment for ferns, mosses, and plants such as the opposite-leaved saxifrage. In spring more vibrant flowers add a splash of colour. This is a good woodland for wood anemone, wood sorrel, greater stitchwort, dog violet, red campion, lesser celandine, wild garlic and bluebells, but it is the overall setting that makes the place so special.

Industry is not just a thing of the past in this area. The railway that passes the length of the valley has transported china clay down to Par on much the same route as Treffry once created. Another industry ages many species of wildlife. Associated with charcoal-burning is the coppicing of trees – a technique that creates a wider diversity of species in the woodland, since it establishes a varied range of development among the trees in a wood, providing open glades for insects as well as more mature trees for creatures such as the dormouse.

If you should choose to walk as far as St Blazey it is worth looking out for a couple of dragonflies along the river. The beautiful demoiselle and golden-ringed dragonfly both specialize in breeding along slow-moving rivers rather than the standing water preferred by the rest of their families. The wet meadow alongside the river here is good for flag iris and cuckoo flower.

One of our most beautiful flowers, the bluebell grows in the Luxulyan Valley.

that continues in the woodland is that of creating charcoal. Thankfully this is one business that does no harm to the ecosystem: in fact it positively encour-

---

LOOK OUT FOR

April–May: In the damp meadows beside the river there is cuckoo flower; dog violets line the hedgerows; greater stitchwort, wild garlic, bluebell, wood anemone and wood sorrel are all common. Look out for the orange tip butterfly here.

June–August: Beautiful demoiselle and golden-ringed dragonfly along the leats. Bats, including the greater horseshoe, occur here. Bilberry is a common plant of the under-storey, and butterflies including the speckled wood and silver-washed fritillary occur in the woodland clearings.

All year: Great spotted woodpecker, green woodpecker, mistle thrush, jay, nuthatch, marsh tit, long-tailed tit, raven, sparrowhawk, buzzard, dipper and grey wagtail; badger.

30

Nature reserve

Explorer 106; *Landranger* 200

By road: Turn off A30 at roundabout near Indian Queens; follow signs for Screech Owl Sanctuary, turning R on to old A30. Park in lay-by on L before railway bridge

SW 933 599

500 ha/1,250 a

Open-ended

3 hours

Rough track, wet in places

Wet heath, dry heath, open water, willow scrub

Gateway from disused railway line SW 938 596; approx centre of Moor SW 951 602

NNR, SAC, SSSI

NE

All year

Free

T: 01872 265 710 (NE, Truro)

Indian Queens

Goss Moor

Goss Moor is an enigma. There can be very few people associated in any way with Cornwall who haven't heard of it or driven across it, but how many of us know anything about it? Even after looking at a map it isn't clear where to start an exploration, but there are good tracks across the moor, and it is excellent for wildlife, so there is no excuse to drive straight past.

Some suggest that Goss Moor was originally named 'Goose Moor' because commoners had, and still have, the right to graze geese on the common land, but I suspect that the more likely explanation is that the word *goss* is Cornish for sedge, and 'moor' is often used as an equivalent for a marsh, so Goss Moor literally means 'sedge marsh'.

Goss Moor nowadays has the feeling of a wilderness: its area is vast and its terrain difficult, but the tracks, signs and remains of buildings hint at some of our previous uses of the area. The earliest signs of work are of tin-streaming in Roman times, but this sort of work continued on an ever-expanding scale, to reach a peak in the eighteenth and nineteenth centuries. At the beginning of the twentieth century the Goss Moor Company assessed that there was approximately 3 lbs of tin per ton of alluvium, and set about recovering this using large dredging machinery – an unprecedented technique in Cornwall. Even at that time tin ore was worth over one shilling per pound, and it is still possible to appreciate that this was a significant value. However, the dredging failed to turn in a profit, and since that time the only work that has taken place is some dredging of gravel, during the Second World War, from the pools which are visible today.

These workings have helped to create the environment we see today, though standing water is

Foxgloves grow on Goss Moor.

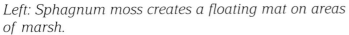

Left: Sphagnum moss creates a floating mat on areas of marsh.
Top: The dark purple flower of the marsh cinquefoil is often difficult to find.
Above: The bog pimpernel grows on damp ground among tussocks of grass.
Right: Bogbean can be found at the edges of pools.

increasingly difficult to see in places where coarse vegetation is taking hold. This is a magical habitat, much of it untouched for almost a century – an area once mastered by our forebears now reclaimed by nature.

My suggested route on to the moor begins near Indian Queens. Follow the small path from the road west of the railway bridge, alongside the railway line and on to the disused section of railway. This spot has the only inland Cornish colony of the grizzled skipper butterfly, and is excellent for southern marsh orchid and wild strawberry, as well as a selection of train-blown plants such as rosebay willowherb and buddleia. (It is likely that the train line was also responsible for the introduction of the grizzled skippers here from the coast.)

The harvest mouse lives on Goss Moor.

A few hundred yards along this old railway there is a track to the left with a padlocked gate. Access on foot can be made around this gate and on to the moor. Take an Ordnance Survey map and explore, but leaving the main tracks is not recommended: there are dangerous areas where floating plants grow on top of water in the pits left behind by tin streamers, which can look like firm ground.

Sphagnum moss is the first species to take hold in these wet areas. This moss acts like a giant sponge, soaking up deluges of rain and releasing the water slowly as conditions dry up. Since Goss Moor is the source of the River Fal, this sphagnum

moss is helping to prevent flooding through many small villages on the way down to the Fal Estuary. However, sphagnum moss is not just part of our flood prevention scheme, it is also a starting point for the production of peat. Initially it creates a stable substrate in which other plant species can take hold, and on Goss Moor there are some attractive flowers, such as bogbean, bog pimpernel and marsh cinque-foil, doing just that. Each year the vegetation grows up, dies back, and gradually builds up layer on layer. The weight of the upper layers, combined with the lack of oxygen in the lower layers, provides ideal conditions for the production of peat. Until recently

The golden-ringed dragonfly frequents slow-flowing rivers.

wintering birds include snipe, water rail and many wildfowl, whereas breeding birds include nightjar and Dartford warbler, which both show a preference for the drier heath to the east of the reserve. The nightjar has a silent and buoyant flight, almost like a butterfly, but it rarely emerges until it is almost dark. It has a most peculiar churring call, which contains no fewer than 1,900 notes per minute, and it is noticeable from great distances. The Dartford warbler has a scratchy call, a little reminiscent of a whitethroat, and lives in gorse thickets throughout the year. It is one of our few resident warblers.

Interesting mammals are also present in good numbers. Harvest mice have been recorded; red deer are increasing in number, and the roe deer is relatively plentiful but difficult to see. Dragonflies are well represented, with as many as 18 species resident, including the small red damselfly. All of Cornwall's amphibians (palmate newt, common toad and common frog), and most of our reptiles (common lizard, adder and slow worm), can also be found here.

sphagnum moss had other uses too: in the First World War it was used as a dressing for wounds – not only is it very absorbent, but it also contains antiseptic ingredients.

The damp grassland provides good growing conditions for devil's bit scabious, which is the food plant of the marsh fritillary butterfly's caterpillar. This butterfly is one of the critical species of Goss Moor since it is globally very rare. The marsh fritillary lives only on the western fringe of Europe, along the Atlantic coast, in wet heaths. As well as needing devilsbit scabious, marsh fritillaries like areas where the marsh is protected from winds by willow scrub, so a mosaic of habitats is best, and that is certainly true of Goss Moor.

Apart from the marsh fritillary, this National Nature Reserve attracts a wide range of wildlife. Special

LOOK OUT FOR

May–June: Grizzled skipper on the old railway line; marsh fritillary, small pearl-bordered fritillary, silver-studded blue butterfly. Marsh orchid, common tway-blade, ragged robin, cotton grass, bogbean, flag iris, bog asphodel, marsh cinquefoil, royal fern and bog pimpernel.

June–July: Nightjar (evenings). Look out for sundew in the damp patches of bare earth.

May–August: Breeding birds including grasshopper warbler, garden warbler, willow warbler and sedge warbler.

Winter: Wildfowl, water rail, snipe, possible birds of prey such as hen harrier and short-eared owl.

All year: Dartford warbler, barn owl and willow tit; sphagnum moss.

31

Nature reserve

Explorer 107; *Landranger* 200

By road: From A30 at Innis Downs roundabout take A391 towards Bugle; after 0.5 ml turn L. Take first R, signed Luxulyan. Stay on road keeping R at next junction; turn L, signed Gunwen. Follow this road approx 1 ml. Park opposite chapel in Lowertown. For entrance to reserve, walk S along this minor road approx 180 m (200 yd), then take track L. Footpath to Helman Tor and reserve

SX 053 613

53 ha/134 a

2 ml

2 hours

First part of reserve quite easy; circular path gets quite difficult

Wetland, woodland, open water, willow carr, heathland, grassland

Boardwalk pond-dipping platform SX 056 612

AGLV, LNR, SAC, SSSI

CWT

All year

Free

T: 01872 273 939 (CWT)

Luxulyan

Breney Common

There are times when, at a superficial level, Breney Common can seem rather lifeless, because the wildlife activity is often played out on a small scale. But visit Breney on a warm summer's day, and you won't fail to witness a plethora of activity and a splash of vibrant colour, as well as some rather macabre goings on.

Although the reserve is a difficult one to find, once there it is a simple matter to follow the circular walk named the Wilderness Trail. Though the name of the trail might suggest a long walk through uncharted territory, nothing could be further from the truth. The area has long been associated with human activity. Historical mining operations here have resulted in an increased diversity of wildlife through the creation of ponds, around which a range of wetland habitats and their associated plants, both common and rare, have flourished. It is now recognized as a nationally important site, consisting of a wonderful mixture of habitats.

The trail passes through all the major habitats on the reserve, the most interesting of which are the meadows where some of the butterflies can be found, and the wet areas, including one pond with a pond-dipping platform. This boardwalk jetty allows the observer to get close to the dragonflies, such as the emperor and four-spotted chaser, which use the centre of the pond.

One of the most significant residents of the reserve is the marsh fritillary butterfly – an important species because it is internationally very rare, and its habitat is threatened. One of the requirements of this butterfly is a healthy population of devilsbit scabious, which is the food plant of its caterpillars. It has been found that to encourage this plant, the

The pond-dipping jetty at Breney.

Left: The marsh fritillary butterfly is an important species found in large numbers at Breney.
Right: The four-spotted chaser is common here during July.

land should be grazed rather than mown. Grazing provides a greater diversity of micro-habitats rather than cutting everything down to the same level. It needs to be performed at a fairly low density, so that grasses are controlled while not destroying the surrounding vegetation. In this instance it has been found that sheep are not the most appropriate grazing animals, since they seem to prefer devilsbit scabious to grass, so at Breney the Wildlife Trust uses horses for this purpose.

Attacks by parasitic wasps can have a major effect on the population of marsh fritillaries at any one site so, being a fairly sedentary species, it is important to offer the butterfly many suitable locations within easy reach, so that their overall numbers can be maintained. This is one reason why the large wildlife complex consisting of Breney, Redmoor, Goss and Tregoss moors is so important within Cornwall.

At Breney there are two good places to look for marsh fritillaries. The first is before entering the reserve proper. To the right of the track leading from the road on to the reserve there is a kissing gate. Go through there and you will find a damp meadow alongside a small stream. The second is in the large meadow situated on the circular walk – the fritillaries favour the area in the shelter of the trees. The critical factor with these butterflies is time of year – there is no point in looking for them outside their flight season in late May and June. A second factor to consider is the weather, since fritillaries are active

Grass snakes live where there is plenty of water and vegetation.

only when there is sun, and they are easiest to watch when it is calm.

Other species of butterfly which attract attention at Breney are the small pearl-bordered fritillary and the silver-studded blue, but there are also a great many dragonflies and damselflies around the ponds and streams. A wide range of species can be seen, some of the most exciting of which are the small red damselfly, black darter, emperor dragonfly and four-spotted chaser. The descriptive names of these species say much about the appearance of these colourful insects, but there is no substitute for seeing them in the flesh.

At the edges of the wetter areas of the reserve keep an eye out for a slithering in the grass. Unlike in the majority of the county, where adders are the commoner snake, here we are much more likely to see a grass snake. A grass snake will take frogs and newts, and is quite capable of swimming in pursuit of its prey. Though the grass snake will grow to be much larger than an adder, it is absolutely harmless to us, so don't be alarmed if you see one.

One of the more obvious flowers in the reeds is the flag iris; the unmistakable yellow flowers are in stark contrast to the more subtle colours of some of the less common species. A flower that I enjoy seeing here is the marsh cinquefoil – no need for an explanation of the name of that species; this specialist of acidic bogs has five very distinctive dark purple petals. Also growing in and around the wet areas, the royal fern unrolls its statuesque fronds for the summer: the rich colour of its foliage makes it our most easily recog-

Left: The royal fern has a distinctively shaped frond.
Right: Cotton grass grows in the marshy ground at Breney.

nized fern. One species whose impact depends to some extent on its multitude is the cotton grass: there can be few other grasses that can compete with a throng of white cottony seed heads blowing in the breeze.

Not all the residents of Breney are pretty and benign. Growing low down on the damp, bare, peaty ground is a secretive and macabre plant. Being named rather flatteringly as the sundew makes this plant sound quite attractive, but the 'dew' refers to sticky globules adorning the plant's leaves. Although the sundew is perfectly harmless to us, it takes its nutrients by trapping unfortunate insects in the sticky

'dew'. Once caught, the insects have little chance as the sundew's flattened leaves begin to curl up around the unfortunate prey, and gradually the plant literally makes a meal of it.

So when you visit Breney, if it seems a little quiet, don't be fooled – take a closer look and you might find more than you bargained for.

The sundew (this is an oblong-leaved sundew) makes a sticky trap for insects.

LOOK OUT FOR

January–February: Frogs and toads begin spawning.

March–April: Palmate newts are at their most active.

April–May: Probably the best time for grass snakes in the waterside vegetation.

Late May–June: Interesting plants include southern marsh orchid, ragged robin, cotton grass, royal fern, lousewort, milkwort, pillwort, broad buckler fern, marsh cinquefoil and sundew. Marsh fritillaries, small pearl-bordered fritillaries and silver-studded blue butterflies become active on sunny days.

June–September: Around the ponds, dragonflies can be exceedingly numerous – this is one of the best sites in Cornwall for this group of insects. Species seen include damselflies (small red, large red, common blue, azure, emerald, blue-tailed and beautiful demoiselle) and dragonflies (golden-ringed, emperor, four-spotted chaser, broad-bodied chaser, common darter and black darter).

August–September: Heather in flower.

Resident: Great spotted and green woodpeckers, long-tailed tit, bullfinch and willow tit.

e of location	Country house and estate, walk on public rights of way
map	*Explorer* 107; *Landranger* 200
directions to start point	By road: From A30 near Bodmin take turn towards Liskeard on A38 and follow signs
starting point	SX 099 636
size	400 ha/1,000 a
length	Approx 4 ml
ended time	2 hours + time for house, gardens
conditions	Good quality footpaths; wheelchair access along river and some areas of estate and gardens
habitats	Woodland, parkland, river, meadow, garden
s of interest	Respryn Bridge SX 099 635; house SX 085 636; estate offices SX 089 641
owner	NT
open	Estate: All year, all times
entry	Estate: Free. House, formal gardens: Charge for non-members
enquiries	T: 01208 742 81 (NT, Lanhydrock)
site facilities	

Lanhydrock

There can be few residents of Cornwall who have not heard of, or indeed visited, Lanhydrock. The fabulous house and its associated gardens, owned by the National Trust since 1953, are a well-known historical attraction, but since Cornwall has few large areas of parkland we should also celebrate the wonderful flora and fauna that the surrounding estate has to offer.

To understand the area we must look to the medieval period when the land here belonged to the priory of St Petroc at Bodmin. At that time it was heavily wooded, but the intensification of farming meant that many trees were felled to make way for agriculture. Once the house had been purchased by the Robartes family in 1620, the estate was developed as a deer park, and many ornamental features were added, including a spring-fed swimming pool and a ha-ha. The first trees used to form avenues, similar to those that we see today, were sycamores, planted in 1648 to commemorate the end of the civil war. In the early nineteenth century they were replaced by beech trees, which are now a characteristic feature of Lanhydrock. Since then there has been little change to the landscape, except for a period during the Second World War when the land was ploughed for the production of food.

One unfortunate feature of many country estates is the preponderance of laurel and rhododendron. These shrubs were introduced for their bold colours, and as cover for game birds such as pheasants, but they become invasive, forming permanent, dense canopies under which none of our indigenous flora can flourish. At Lanhydrock the National Trust has been working hard to eradicate these pernicious intruders, and it is reassuring to see that where the

Lanhydrock House is situated in a large parkland habitat.

Above: One of the finest bluebell woods in Cornwall is situated near the entrance to Lanhydrock.
Left: Rhododendrons look fine in the formal gardens, but are being removed from the estate.

laurel and rhododendrons have been removed the natural ground flora of the woodlands has recovered within a couple of years.

Other species that are being removed from the estate include larch and spruce trees, both of which are capable of crowding out the magnificent ancient oaks. Where thinning of trees is necessary, for the safety of visitors or for the health of the woodland, decaying wood and piles of brush are left among the trees to provide homes for wood mice and dormice, and places for birds to nest. Many dead trees are left *in situ* to decay naturally, providing nesting sites for woodpeckers and owls, as well as a home for beetles and fungi.

A good circular walk around Lanhydrock starts at the car-park near Respryn Bridge. Follow the River Fowey downstream, then cross the river and head up to the house along the wooded paths. Walk back either along the beech avenue, or up the drive, forking right past the estate offices. This attractive path leads through another woodland before returning along the minor road to Respryn Bridge.

Before starting out on this route, have a look at the damp meadow just upstream of the car-park at Respryn Bridge. This is an attractive place for cuckoo flower, and during April and May there is a good chance of seeing some of our earliest butter-flies, such as the orange tip and brimstone. The path along the river is a gentle one, usually offering great views of dippers and grey wagtails. Look for them on the rocks in the riverbed. Also along here it is often possible to see treecreepers – they thrive in the damp atmosphere of the riverside, and seem to enjoy having their trees lined up neatly ready for exploration. Watch as the treecreeper climbs a tree by spiralling upwards around its trunk before flying down to land near the foot of an adjacent one, and starting the process again.

There is a choice of paths from the small foot-bridge leading up to the house, but all pass through woodland rich in spring flowers. In early May blue-bells are dominant, growing in great swathes. These woods are one of the best in the county for this wonderful flower. Other species growing here include wild garlic, wood sorrel, wood anemone, and a few early purple orchids. In April, where hedge banks are exposed to the sun, look for the diminutive holly blue butterfly basking on the foliage. This silvery-blue butterfly not only feeds on the flowers of holly,

Early purple orchids flower at the same time as bluebells.

Left: A spotted flycatcher often nests in the front garden of the house.
Above: The mistle thrush thrives in parkland.

but also lays its eggs on the holly's leaves where its caterpillars will feed.

By late May the woods should be playing host to a number of warblers and flycatchers, which are not at all common in Cornwall. Look out for garden warbler, redstart, pied flycatcher, and maybe the odd wood warbler, as well as the commoner species such as blackcap and chiffchaff. The other flycatcher – the spotted – is more likely to be seen in the courtyard in front of the house, since it seems to like nesting in the climber there. Look out for it perching on the signposts in the front garden.

Snowdrops grow in the gardens of Lanhydrock.

The formal gardens around the house and church may be a little ornate for the nature-lover, but they are nonetheless very impressive, particularly from April to June. The house is also of great interest, and is well worth a visit.

The house looks out over short grass and mature trees – typical parkland habitat. This is one of the best places to watch, or listen for, the green woodpecker. The mad laugh, or yaffle, of this bird is one of the most characteristic calls of any Cornish bird. Another bird which is most commonly found in this sort of environment is the mistle thrush, and this too has an obvious call, sounding a little like a football rattle. Buzzards are likely to be seen soaring overhead on warm days, along with occasional sparrowhawks.

LOOK OUT FOR

January–February: The show of woodland flowers begins with snowdrops, particularly in the gardens.

February–April: Lesser spotted, great spotted and green woodpeckers establishing their territories around the estate.

April–May: This is one of the best sites in the county for bluebells; also wood sorrel, wood anemone, wild garlic, wood avens, common cow-wheat, primrose, pignut, wood speedwell, hairy woodrush, dog's mercury, enchanter's nightshade and early purple orchid in the woodlands. In the damp meadows, cuckoo flower, orange tip and brimstone butterfly; holly blue butterflies around the hedgerows. Older surveys of the land suggest that wood and marbled white butterflies may also occur here along with silver-washed fritillary and purple hairstreak.

May–June: Pied flycatchers, redstarts and warblers. Watch out for oil beetles on the grassy paths.

June–August: Spotted flycatchers around the house. Insects include various longhorn and ground beetles.

October–November: Good autumnal colour complemented by a variety of fungi (over 500 species recorded) growing on the decaying wood of old trees.

December–January: The trees play host to a wide range of lichens, including one particularly rare species known as lungwort or *Lobaria pulmonaria*, so called because of its resemblance to the structures in the lungs. Look out for this on the path past the estate offices on the way down to the Respryn Bridge car-park.

All year: Dipper, grey wagtail and kingfisher on the river; sparrowhawk, buzzard, tawny owl, nuthatch and treecreeper in the woods.

location	Nature reserve
map	*Explorer* 200; *Landranger* 201
directions to start point	By road: From A38 Bodmin to Liskeard, take minor road L approx 1 ml after turn for Bodmin Parkway Station at SX 131 651. Cross River Fowey, turn R on small track. Park by sawmill or by roadside
starting point	SX 129 653
size	77 ha/190 a
length	3 ml
needed time	3 hours
conditions	Some tracks, some footpaths, can be muddy
habitats	Woodland, river
of interest	Sawmill SX 129 653; wood pasture, centred on SX 132 652
designation	LNR
owner	CWT
open	All year
entry	Free
enquiries	T: 01872 273 939 (CWT)
facilities	Bodmin
facilities	

Cabilla and Redrice

Cornwall is not a county renowned for its woodland: the influence of the elements caused by its geographical position is not conducive to the growth of tall trees, except in the most sheltered of areas. The further east we go in the county, the more shelter we find, and the greater the likelihood of there being significant areas of mature trees. Other woodlands featured in this book, such as those at Kilminorth, Luxulyan and Golitha (Sites 34, 29 and 35 respectively) have large trees because they grow in sheltered valleys, but in the Glynn Valley we have the longest stretch of unbroken woodland in the county. Shelter for the trees here is provided by the steep sides of the valley created by the River Fowey, between Bodmin and Liskeard, and the most accessible and interesting section is that known as Cabilla and Redrice Woods.

There are two fundamentally different sections to the reserve: one is the coppiced woodland on the hillsides, and the other is the wood pasture in the valley bottom. Management of the coppiced woodland is a fairly simple, though time-consuming task. Coppicing involves cutting back the trees to near ground level, in such a way as to encourage vigorous new shoots to appear in the following spring. It is because these shoots grow so quickly that this process was first used for producing wood to make charcoal.

At Cabilla the trees are cut on a 20-year rotation to provide different habitats which merge gradually into each other, offering the opportunity for the greatest possible biodiversity. For an example of a group of species that thrive in these conditions, consider the fritillary butterflies. Their caterpillars feed on the leaves of violets which, in turn, thrive in the recently coppiced areas of woodland. As a result of coppicing

The River Fowey flows along the edge of Cabilla Woods.

Left: Silver-washed fritillaries enjoy the summer in woodland clearings.
Right: Many nest boxes have been provided to help the dormouse to prosper.

at Cabilla and Redrice, there are healthy populations of small pearl-bordered and, the much larger, silver-washed fritillaries.

Small rodents are also doing well in the coppiced woodland. Their lives are made easier by the good crop of hazelnuts in the autumn, and by the nest boxes erected primarily to help dormice. The dormouse is a heavily protected species, and must not be disturbed at any time of year, with the exception of people licensed to do so. The Wildlife Trust has a regular monitoring programme for dormice, to make sure that they are responding well to conservation work. The dormouse – whose name comes from the French word *dormir* – does a lot of sleeping; in fact it was once commonly known as 'the sleeper'. It hibernates from October to March in a hole in the ground, and then enters a state of torpor throughout

the daylight hours of summer. At dusk, dormice everywhere emerge to feed, before going back to sleep when they are full.

When the Wildlife Trust took on the reserve in 1997, the wood pasture around the river's flood plain had become completely overgrown, so resurrecting the quality of this habitat has been a time-consuming task. Up until the middle of the last century it was an open area, with oak trees dominating over grassland. The pasture was grazed, and so scrub was kept at bay. In the mid-1950s the grazing ceased, and a woodland under-storey soon grew and began to overtake the oak trees, depriving them of light.

Simply cutting back the shrubs of the understorey would not have solved the problem, since they would then grow even more rapidly, and the problem would be exacerbated in the long term. The answer

Above: Sparrowhawks can be seen hunting around the woods.
Right: Pied flycatchers can sometimes be found breeding at Cabilla.

was to combine cutting with the use of animals to graze the new shoots as they appeared, but it took a hardy grazer to eke out a living in an area without any lush grass. The Trust opted for Exmoor ponies, and a small group of them now live and graze in the valley bottom, chomping through any new shoots of growth from the tree stumps. After a few years, if the trees can't send up new shoots their stumps begin to rot. Fortunately the ponies are also tackling the tussocks of purple moor grass, which were threatening to overwhelm the areas of woodland as they opened up.

Red deer can be seen in the more remote parts of the woods.

The oak trees of the pasture can now be recognized again as they begin to dominate once more. The old oak trees are so very important to the ecosystem here, and because of their age they are virtually irreplaceable. It can take an oak 500 years to reach old age, but its importance continues for another 500 years as it dies and gradually decays. Species which depend upon the oak, such as lichens which grow on its branches, will be able to thrive once the light begins to penetrate through to them again. There are some unusual and rare insects here that live on the slowly decaying wood of old trees: possibly the most special is the blue ground beetle, which lives only in this specific type of habitat.

One bird that prospers in oak woodland with such clearings is the pied flycatcher. This bird bred only sporadically in Cornwall during the latter half of the twentieth century. Its spread from strongholds in Wales and the North West has been assisted by the provision of nest boxes in Somerset, Devon and now East Cornwall, but its progress into Cornwall has been painfully slow. The woodlands of Cabilla and

In the autumn look out for fungi, including the jelly antler fungus, on decaying logs.

Redrice offer a chance to see one, but only in May and June.

Throughout the year both sparrowhawk and buzzard can be seen soaring on the thermals created over the valley slopes. Being part of a large area of woodland, it should come as no surprise that there are plenty of fungi here in the autumn. Also most noticeable in the autumn are the red deer which live in the valley, for this is the time of year when the stags enter their rut. Red deer are not easy to see in Cornwall, but the Glynn Valley is one of their strongholds. The most widespread of our deer species is the roe deer, and this too can be found here. An early morning walk would be advisable for hopeful deer-watchers: look out for their prints, or slots, in the muddy tracks.

LOOK OUT FOR

April–May: Perhaps the most attractive season, with wood anemone, bluebells, wild garlic and wood sorrel.

April–August: Grass snake, adder, common lizard and slow worm are all resident here.

May–June: Pied flycatchers sometimes breed here, and small pearl-bordered fritillary is present. Dormice are numerous in these woods, but to see them you must attend a guided walk by the Wildlife Trust.

July–August: Butterflies at their best; a good chance of seeing silver-washed fritillaries.

September–October: Best time for seeing red deer.

October–November: Great for fungi in the woods.

All year: Dipper, grey wagtail, nuthatch, siskin, marsh tit, sparrowhawk and buzzard. Roe deer and otter. English and sessile oak.

Kilminorth Woods

Kilminorth Woods, alongside the West Looe River, is a fine example of an ancient western sessile oak wood, and because the trails leading through this nature reserve also meander close to a tidal, muddy creek a wide range of birds and other wildlife can be seen here.

Even before leaving the car-park in West Looe, at the confluence of the East and West Looe Rivers, the action starts. From here there is a wonderfully open view of an active heronry, which must be the most easily watched heronry in Cornwall. The grey herons regularly feed alongside the creek in front of the car-park. If you arrive early in the morning on a low tide, and stay in your car, you will be rewarded with excellent views. As the day progresses and the number of people builds up the herons will stay a little further away, but they can always be watched in the trees. Spring is best, because the birds will be either nest-building or raising young, and the deciduous trees won't yet have developed enough foliage to block the view.

Grey herons give the impression of being at home on the muddy margins of the river, but in the trees they can look cumbersome and ungainly. The thought of such a bird building a nest of twigs and branches at the top of a tree seems fantastic. I often wonder how birds get started: how do they get the first few twigs to stay in place while they knit in the next? A grey heron's nest is never 'finished', but once it becomes habitable it must cope with wind, rain and the combined mass of adults and young. When the young are born the nest will also need to be resilient enough to survive the arguments and fights that often break out as the precocious youths clamour for their parents' attention.

The oak trees of Kilminorth Woods
hang over the creek.

Left: The path through Kilminorth Woods near Watergate.
Above: Shelduck nest in the woods and can often be seen in the creek.

It is worth setting off early, so that you can walk the three-mile circular route to Watergate before coming back to Looe for a bite of lunch. The welcoming sign at the entrance to the woodland walk reads: 'Jack the Giant, having nothing to do, built a hedge from Lerryn to Looe.' This saying, of which there are many variations, refers to a giant linear earthwork presumed to mark the northern boundary of a post-Roman kingdom. Along the best-preserved sections of this hedge it is nearly two metres high and three and a half metres wide, with a ditch on its northern side. In Kilminorth Woods, where it ends, it reaches a height of two and a half metres, with occasional stone revetments.

The fact that the woodland is classified as 'ancient woodland' means that trees have grown here unin-

Above: Grey herons nest in the trees opposite the car-park.
Right: Kingfishers could be encountered along the creek.

terrupted for 400 years or more, but that doesn't mean that the same trees have been here for all that time. In fact, like so many of Cornwall's trees, these have been managed by people, through a process of coppicing, to produce charcoal; tannin from the oak trees' bark, and wood for boat-building. Though this process originated for human gain it has also proved very useful for wildlife, since it encourages a greater diversity of habitats and a more vibrant growth of ground flora. Though we no longer stand to gain directly from the process of coppicing, in order to conserve this interesting habitat the woods are now managed by rotational coppicing and thinning of invasive species such as sycamore.

Common polypody is just one of the many ferns which grow in the woodland.

From clearings in the wood look up to see soaring birds of prey, such as sparrowhawk and buzzard. Also common here are the ravens which often fly over this valley, croaking with their characteristically gruff voices. Some years they nest in one of the very tall coniferous trees in the woodland so, if you visit in early spring, look out for adult birds flying back and forth to their nest.

Where the path gives views over the muddy estuary, walk slowly to a vantage point to avoid disturbing the birds. Here you should see little egret, shelduck, curlew and oystercatcher, but there could well be other species, such as whimbrel, passing through in spring.

Towards Watergate the river attracts kingfishers, but you will need to be patient or very lucky to see one. The kingfisher flies fast, making it a difficult bird to pick out, but fortunately it does have a distinctive call which it uses frequently in flight. The sound to listen for is a very high-pitched, fairly drawn out, whistling 'peeep'. If you hear it, then look low over the water, because that is where the kingfisher invariably flies. The best you can hope to see is a blue blur. With luck, and if you keep watching, you may see it come to rest on a boat, or on a branch overhanging the river.

Having so far dwelt upon birds, I must add that the flora of this woodland is excellent in spring. There is

The speckled wood butterfly is common around the woodland edge.

Kilminorth Woods provides a gentle place for a relaxing walk, offering a wide range of wildlife in habitats that are diverse yet conveniently placed. One of its beauties is that the trails through these woods offer an excellent chance to combine a wild-life walk with a more conventional family outing to the seaside. It often surprises me how it is possible to get away from the hustle and bustle while remaining in such close proximity to humanity.

the beautiful blue of the bluebell; the subtle yellow of the primrose, and the soft white of wild garlic, but it is the most stunning array of ferns that dominates the understorey here. Their appeal is not just in their sumptuous green colour, but also in the shapes and textures of their fronds as they push through the ground and unfurl into their well-known statuesque mature forms; this is our temperate version of a tropical rainforest.

LOOK OUT FOR

January–May: Good time for watching the grey herons at the heronry, and ravens nesting.

April–May: Excellent time to visit, with many flowers including lesser celandine, wood sorrel and wood anemone in the woodland, and cuckoo flower in the damp, riverside meadows.

May–August: Warm summer days are good for watching buzzards, sparrowhawks and ravens soaring over the valley. Butterflies, such as speckled wood and purple emperor, can be seen in the woodland clearings. Young grey herons learn to hunt in full view of the car-park. Watch shelducks bringing their young down from the woods on to the estuary to feed. Ferns include hard, hartstongue and common polypody; greater woodrush is common.

Autumn–Winter: A variety of wading birds, such as curlew, oystercatcher, redshank and dunlin use the estuary; kingfishers are most likely to be seen in winter, particularly around Watergate.

All year: Great spotted woodpecker, nuthatch and little egret.

site number	**35**
type of location	**Nature reserve**
map	*Explorer* 109; *Landranger* 201
directions to start point	**By road: From A38 at Doublebois take minor road towards Minions; after approx 3 ml turn L, then immediately L again. Park on R over bridge**
starting point	**SX 227 690 (car-park)**
size	**12 ha/30 a**
length	**1.5 ml**
recommended time	**2 hours**
conditions	**Good for short distance, then rocky and difficult**
habitats	**Woodland, river**
points of interest	**For best falls, walk to SX 220 685**
landscape designation	**AONB, NNR**
owner	**NE**
open	**Daily**
entry	**Free**
enquiries	**T: 01872 265 710 (NE, Truro)**
nearest facilities	**St Cleer for shop and pub**
site facilities	

Golitha Falls

Water crashes through the valley, its sound filling the air of the steep-sided gorge. The mist caused by the water's incessant activity hangs in the branches of the oak trees, creating high levels of humidity. Taking advantage of this moisture, a wide range of mosses and ferns grow on the surface of every tree and rock, creating a lush, tactile covering. The scent of the river hangs heavy in the depths of the valley, somehow enriched by the cool, damp air. Saturated colours create a vivid backdrop to the beauty of the river, which ceaselessly batters the cold, hard granite boulders in its bed. Every sense is aroused in the wonderful atmosphere of this National Nature Reserve at Golitha Falls.

This gorge was formed by the River Fowey as it cascaded down from Bodmin Moor. The river follows the joint between granite bedrock to the north and slate to the south, eroding and enlarging the geological weakness between the two. Nature created a much higher waterfall than we see today, but in the nineteenth century a large rock, known as the Golitha Stone, was dynamited to dislodge it, thus making the river more suitable for salmon to migrate along its length.

The human touch has had a much greater influence over the valley than simply the dislodging of a single rock. In the middle of the nineteenth century prospectors found copper ore in the valley, and a great effort was made to mine it. Leats were dug, taking water from further upstream along the side of the river valley to two large water wheels. It is estimated that these wheels were 30 feet in diameter, and the wheel pits are still in good condition today. One of the wheels is known to have driven flat rods

The River Fowey crashes through the Golitha Falls National Nature Reserve.

Above: Liverworts, such as the Pellia epiphylla, *grow at Golitha.*
Left: A spore capsule of the moss Pohlia nutans.

approximately 1,000 feet long, to work a pump in one mine shaft. The copper did not last long, and the shafts that were dug overnight were just as quickly deserted. The overhead pipeline at the top of the falls was built at around the end of the nineteenth century, by the predecessors of the English China Clay company, to carry clay slurry from clay works on Bodmin Moor to a drying facility near Liskeard. The leats have now been utilized as footpaths, and the

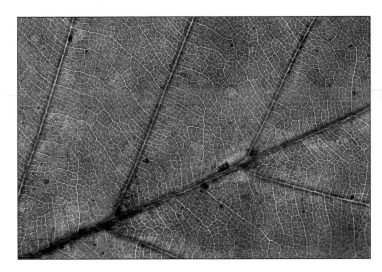

Above: The colourful leaf of a beech tree in autumn.
Right: The flowers of lesser celandine can be seen
from March to May.

old adits and shafts are used by bats – most notably the lesser horseshoe bat.

The obvious and indisputable beauty of this ancient sessile oak woodland is not the reason for its selection as a National Nature Reserve, though it is probably the reason for its popularity. It is the ferns and bryophytes which make this valley so special. Ferns are specially adapted to life on the woodland floor: their leaves or fronds push through the debris of leaf litter, many forming the shape of a shepherd's crook before unrolling to reveal a very large surface area to gather as much light as possible in this relatively dark environment. Of the ferns present at Golitha, the Tunbridge Filmy Fern is the least common. Its fronds are unlike most ferns, and look more like seaweed.

The term bryophyte is derived from the Latin word *bryophyta*, which in turn came from the Greek words *bruon*, meaning moss, and *phuton*, meaning plant. It is now used as the collective name for the mosses and liverworts. There are approximately 1,000 species of

Above: Honey fungus is common on the trees at Golitha.
Right: The great spotted woodpecker lives in this wooded valley. This is a male.

bryophyte in Britain, many of which can be named by only a very few specialists, but their beauty can be appreciated by us all. Encouraged by the increased humidity of the river valley, and the quality of the air, they grow prolifically here.

Many more sophisticated plants and animals also live on this reserve. In spring the beech trees, intro-duced here, unfurl their delicate, translucent leaves, allowing dappled light to reach the woodland floor, where bluebells, lesser celandine and other spring woodland flowers grow. As summer approaches, butterflies begin to make use of the small fields on the northern edge of the woodland. Here species such as the silver-washed fritillary and speckled

wood butterfly find nectar in the many flowers, and sunlight in which to bask.

Throughout the year, dippers and grey wagtails can be seen along the course of the river. Higher up the valley slopes, pied flycatchers can be found nesting from May to July. Resident throughout the year are the more typical woodland birds, such as great spotted woodpecker, nuthatch and treecreeper.

Also present here, though very difficult to see, is the otter. This secretive animal thrives in the clean water of the River Fowey. Its presence is revealed by the spraints which it leaves in strategic positions around its territory. Among other mammals using the woodland and leaving tracks to reveal their presence are foxes and badgers.

LOOK OUT FOR

March–May: Woodland flowers such as lesser celandine, wood anemone, wood sorrel and bluebell.

May–June: Nesting birds include buzzard, dipper, grey wagtail, pied flycatcher, nuthatch and treecreeper.

June–August: Flora include greater woodrush, bilberry, hard fern, wavy-hair grass and common cow-wheat. The silver-washed fritillary and speckled wood butterfly can be seen in glades.

October–November: Fungi – especially common are the honey fungus and stump mycena; the autumnal colour is among the best in Cornwall.

November–February: The best season for looking at lichens: the beech trees play host to some interesting species.

All year: Around 50 species of liverwort, and 98 species of moss.

Country park

map

Explorer 108; *Landranger* 201

ections to
start point

By road: From Callington take A390 towards Gunnislake; after approx 1 ml turn L, then first L marked Kit Hill. Car-parks on hill

ting point

SX 375 714

size

160 ha/400 a

length

Circular walk, following stack stones, approx 2 ml

nded time

2 hours

conditions

Often rocky and difficult

habitats

Heathland, pond, wetland

of interest

Kit Hill Quarry SX 374 717; folly SX 375 713; South Kit Hill mine SX 374 709; wolfram adits SX 380 715; Luckett village car-park SX 389 737; Greenscombe Woods SX 392 726

esignation

AONB

owner

CCC

open

All year

enquiries

T: 01872 222 000
(CCC, Environment Service)

t facilities

Café signed on route, or Callington

e facilities

Kit Hill

The large granite intrusion which is Kit Hill stands some 333 metres above sea level, and some 200 metres proud of the neighbouring landscape. Its grandiose stature might be humbled by the distant hills of Dartmoor and Bodmin Moor, which can be admired from its summit, but because it stands proud of its immediate surroundings it forms an easily recognizable beacon for all around.

The earliest human activity here is likely to have been attracted by the shape and size of the hill, which must have made it an important ritual site. Evidence of this is in the form of barrows, or burial mounds. There are examples of a Neolithic long barrow (*c.* 3000 BC), and Bronze Age barrows (*c.* 2000 BC). In the late medieval period there was some tin-streaming and quarrying on the slopes of the hill. In the late eighteenth century, it was once again the shape of the hill that attracted attention, when Sir John Call built a huge folly on the summit. The folly commemorated the nearby battle of Hingston Down in AD 838, when the Anglo Saxon King Egbert decided to challenge the Cornish resistance.

In around 1820 mining became dominant in the landscape. First Kit Hill Mine, with its wind-powered engine, and then South Kit Hill Mine, with shafts to a depth of 300 feet, extracted copper and wolfram from the hill. On the eastern slopes it is easy to see where adits were dug to extract wolfram – an element used to harden steel – from close to the surface as recently as 1918. More recent industry on the hill includes the quarrying of granite, with its associated inclined railways, the tracks of which are still visible on the north side of the hill. This ended in 1955.

A view from Kit Hill.

Above: Gorse is a feature of the hill and begins to flower in winter.
Left: The Dartford warbler is a rare and very secretive bird which breeds on the hill.

Several thousand years ago the hill would have been lightly wooded, but grazing has been a feature here since Neolithic times, and gradually the trees were eradicated. The poor soils associated with mining have allowed heathland species, such as heather and gorse, to encroach to a point where this is now the dominant habitat.

Heathland is not a climax habitat. This means that if left alone it would eventually revert to woodland by a natural succession of species, from heather, to gorse, to rowan, to ash, and eventually to oak.

It may be that Kit Hill was named after the buzzard!

Letting nature take its course may seem to be the best thing to do, and a small area of the hill is indeed being left to develop in this way, but conservationists like to conserve the many and varied habitats that we now have in our countryside. The buzz word is biodiversity. In order to conserve heathland it needs to be grazed, so grazing rights on the hill are let to local farmers.

Cattle alone probably wouldn't be able to keep the coarse vegetation at bay, so some work is undertaken to control the gorse. Since the hill is such a significant feature in the surrounding landscape, the method of cutting is applied sensitively, creating a mosaic of different levels of growth rather than linear tracts. In contrast, on the south-west side of the hill, we can see an area of heathland that was converted to 'improved grassland' in the 1970s. Encouraged by agricultural grants at that time, the land was fertilized and grazed heavily, creating a sterile monoculture of grass.

It is thought that the name of the hill was derived from the term 'Kite's Hill', and although there is a kite species resident in Britain, it is more likely that the kite in question was the 'fuzz kite' – an old name for the common buzzard still very much in evidence today.

Living among the furze, or gorse, on this heathland are some delightful species of birds, including a few pairs of Dartford warbler. This is typically a bird of the Mediterranean region, but the warming

Redwings arrive on the hill in October and can be see here through the winter.

climate has enabled it to spread to our shores. It enjoys the safety afforded by the dense thickets of gorse on the hill, and is now well established. Though very shy, the Dartford warbler does have a distinctive scratchy song, which should enable observers to locate it – approximately! Even when pinned down to an area of gorse bushes it might still prove elusive. More obvious are the stonechats, which always perch out in the open, and their stone-tapping chat calls are as persistent as any of Cornwall's birds.

The shape and size of the hill is not lost on our wildlife. At times of migration, birds use geographical features to help them remember their route, so hills like this often act as beacons, and many birds stop off to feed here. Among the heather and grasses on top of the hill watch out for pipits, finches, buntings and larks. In the sheltered quarry look for warblers.

If you are visiting Kit Hill in June, I suggest a diversion to nearby Greenscombe Wood. A couple of miles to the north-east of Kit Hill is the village of Luckett, and it is a short walk from here into the woods. This woodland is special because it is one of the sites where heath fritillary butterflies have been reintroduced.

in June. There are information panels in the wood giving details, and you should look for the butterflies in the clearings of the deciduous woodland, where there is plenty of cow-wheat and plantain, which are the food plants of the heath fritillary's caterpillars.

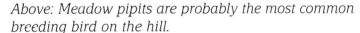
Above: Meadow pipits are probably the most common breeding bird on the hill.
Right: The heath fritillary butterfly has been reintroduced at Greenscombe, near Kit Hill.

This rare butterfly once lived here, and its population was used to reintroduce them to a site near Lydford in Devon. Since then the population at Greenscombe died out, due to poor management of the environment, but fortunately the Lydford group thrived. Subsequently, having corrected the management of the woods, eggs from the Lydford area have been raised in captivity and released at Greenscombe. Literally thousands of these beautiful little butterflies, found at only a handful of sites in Britain, have been released here, and they can be seen on the wing

LOOK OUT FOR

Spring–Autumn: Good for watching migrant birds, which occasionally include ring ouzel, redstart and hobby.

Summer: Dragonflies are numerous in the quarry. Flowers include hedge bedstraw, foxglove, cotton grass, common centaury, bilberry and broom. Willow warblers nest in the scrub.

August–September: Bell heather, ling and cross-leaved heath flower, along with western gorse.

Winter: Large numbers of meadow pipits, skylarks, redwings and fieldfares.

All year: Stonechat and Dartford warbler live in the areas of gorse; other numerous birds include yellowhammer, linnet, skylark, jay, great spotted woodpecker, bullfinch and kestrel; raven and buzzard live and breed on the hill. Roe deer live here, but you need to be early to see them.

Nature reserve

Explorer 108; *Landranger* 201

By road: Take A390 from Callington towards Gunnislake; turn R just before St Ann's Chapel, signed Donkey Sanctuary. Turn L immediately after Donkey Sanctuary. Park by side of road by a footpath on L (sign to Rifle Volunteer Inn). Access reserve by walking a few metres up path on L

SX 413 707

5 ha/12 a

1 hour

Easy walking on grass

Meadow

LNR, SSSI

CWT

On set days during June (contact CWT)

Free

T: 01872 273 939 (CWT)

St Ann's Chapel

Sylvia's Meadow

Sylvia's Meadow is simply the best place in Cornwall to see orchids. It is thought to contain seven species within its five-hectare boundary.

It is interesting to look at the history of this small meadow to understand why it is such a rich site for orchids when the fields around it have relatively few. The meadow may well have been used for agriculture in the distant past, but at the time when the use of chemicals in farming became so prevalent this site was protected, not by being a nature reserve, but through being an American base in the Second World War. Apparently two fields were used by the Americans: astonishingly, one was for its white men and the other for its black recruits. When most of our land was being ploughed and planted as part of the war effort, this field was saved. After the war, when chemicals were used even more heavily in agriculture, the buildings in this field were converted into a cinema, and a pattern of public use began to develop. The meadow was named after the daughter of a previous owner, but it has been owned by the Cornwall Wildlife Trust since 1992.

When the Wildlife Trust first took over the meadow, it was not the plough that threatened the orchids but the lack of grazing. Orchids, like other flowers in a meadow, are threatened by the dominance of the grasses among which they grow. Without regular grazing, longer grass and then scrub would grow up and smother the flowers, preventing them from germinating. At first, grazing was carried out by the donkeys of the Tamar Donkey Park, which is conveniently situated in the next field, but more recently the Wildlife Trust has turned to sheep to do this job, because the donkeys were a little choosy in

Sylvia's Meadow is a simple field,
but with a complex flora.

SYLVIA'S MEADOW

Should you have any
concern regarding
The Donkeys

Please contact us on :
Tel 01822 834072

THANK YOU
THE TAMAR VALLEY DONKEY PARK
info@donkeypark.com
www.donkeypark.com

The establishment of
this Reserve has been
made possible with the
support of the National
Heritage Memorial Fund.
British Telecom. Caradon
District Council.
ARC South Western.
Local people and
businesses during 1992.

CORNWALL LANDSCAPE
PROJECT

Left: A greater butterfly orchid in close-up reveals the angled pollen clumps.
Above: Lesser butterfly orchids are by far the commoner of the two species of butterfly orchids.

what they ate, and were concentrating their efforts on the lush grass where the orchids grow, leaving the coarser vegetation untouched. The level and type of grazing is quite important. There is no doubt that orchids grow taller where the surrounding vegetation is taller, but if the vegetation is too dense or insurmountable, the orchids won't even show their heads. Getting the balance right is a challenge.

Most orchids are undeniably beautiful. Like the grasses which surround them in the meadow, they are monocotyledons, so orchids have simple, narrow leaves with parallel veins. However, unlike the grasses, which have inconspicuous flowers and large seeds, orchids have ornate flowers and very small seeds. The reason for these two differences is that grasses have evolved to be pollinated by the wind,

Left: The southern marsh orchid is our commonest species of orchid.
Right: Heath spotted orchids are much paler than the other pink orchids.

whereas orchids are designed to be pollinated by insects.

The challenge when faced with a variety of orchids is to distinguish between them, and this is no mean feat. Part of the problem with identification is that the similar species are regularly cross-polli-nated, creating hybrids. So when you think you've mastered the common spotted orchid and the heath spotted orchid, you come to Sylvia's Meadow and find a million and one orchids that could be either!

One or two of the key orchids at Sylvia's Meadow have some characteristics that make them easy to

identify. For example, there are the two types of butterfly orchids that occur here, known as greater and lesser butterfly orchids. In general, across much of southern Britain, the greater butterfly orchid is more common than the lesser, but here at Sylvia's Meadow the opposite is true. Named 'butterfly' orchids because of the ornate shape of each of their many flowers, both of these species are creamy white with long flower spurs. The greater butterfly orchid has larger flowers than the lesser, but to be certain about identification close inspection is necessary. In the flower of the lesser butterfly orchid, the two pollen clumps lie parallel to each other, and close together, whereas in the greater butterfly orchid they lie at an angle, and further apart.

June is the best month to visit the reserve, but before June gets under way one orchid – the early purple orchid – will have finished flowering. The early purple orchid has a deep purple colour, and a loose flower spike with spots on its leaves.

At the beginning of June orchids are literally lining up to flower. The southern marsh orchid, very common here, has a more pinky-purple flower than the early purple orchid, and this occurs on a stout stem with a good solid, dense head of flowers. Close inspection usually reveals unspotted leaves, though there is some variation.

The common spotted orchid which, despite its name, is uncommon in Cornwall and not at all numerous even at Sylvia's Meadow, has a longer, often narrower flower spike than the southern marsh orchid, though its flowers are equally dense on the stem. It has a lighter pink flower with a dark pink pattern on each one, and very dark spotting on the leaves.

The final orchid likely to be seen here in June is the heath spotted orchid, a species which is very closely

Left: Yellow rattle grows in the meadow.
Right: A common blue butterfly goes to roost on a southern marsh orchid.

related to the common spotted orchid. In Cornwall the heath spotted is widespread, being found on a great many of our coastal heaths. Its flowers are similar to those of the common spotted orchid, but are a paler pink, verging on white, with a lovely pattern of darker pink spots.

Among the orchids at Sylvia's Meadow are many other species of flowering plant. One of them, the yellow rattle, is a very helpful flower to have in a wildflower meadow. The yellow rattle – so named because it has yellow flowers and its seed-heads sound like a rattle when shaken – is a semi-parasitic species, taking some of its nutrients from the roots of grasses. This direct competition helps to inhibit the growth of the grasses.

If you visit Sylvia's Meadow at any time other than June, you could be forgiven for thinking that this is just a simple, attractive but not very special, Cornish meadow. Arrive here in mid-June and you will realize that this small field is one of the most important of its kind in the country, not just the county.

LOOK OUT FOR

It is only really practical, and most desirable, to visit in **June** when it should be possible to see: marsh orchids, common spotted orchids, maybe some late-flowering early purple orchids, heath spotted orchids, lesser butterfly and greater butterfly orchids. Other flowers common here in June include sneezewort, yellow rattle, devilsbit scabious, milkwort, lousewort, tormentil, sorrel, plantain, buttercup, red campion, clover and flag iris. Butterflies that can readily be seen include a large number of common blue butterflies; wall brown, orange tip, marbled white and dingy skippers may also be found.

Cotehele

The National Trust has owned Cotehele House since 1947, and with it came a very large estate with a great diversity of habitats. Of the land, about six hectares are formal gardens; 105 hectares are mature, often ancient woodland; four hectares are reed-bed and riverbank; the rest is tenanted farmland, used primarily for market gardening, flower growing and some grazing of cattle.

Around the estate, mostly close to the River Tamar and its tributaries, are many buildings and features of historical interest. They include Cotehele Mill, Cotehele Quay, the Chapel in the Wood, the mines of Danescombe Valley, and the ruins of Danescombe's Sawmill and Papermill. The gardens and mill are open only at specified times, but the rest of the estate is accessible through a good selection of public rights of way, paths and tracks.

After parking at the quay, have a look in the lime-kilns. Here you will see a mass of the rare maiden-hair fern. The name of this species seems appropriate when it is seen cascading beautifully from the sides of the kilns. Field guides describe it as found 'growing on limestone sea cliffs', but here the deposits of lime over the centuries have created the correct conditions for it to grow. Even so, I often wonder how it found its way here.

The reed-beds along the River Tamar, close to the quay, offer an uncommon habitat in Cornwall, and an ecology that is totally different from the rest of the estate. The most obvious residents are reed and sedge warblers in summer, and reed buntings all year round. Otters use the stream in the Morden Valley, and no doubt have holts in the reeds where they can enjoy total isolation from people, for they are seldom seen.

*Many varieties of daffodils are being
protected at Cotehele.*

Left: Maidenhair fern hangs from the walls of the lime-kilns at the quay.
Above: The view from Cotehele towards Calstock over the River Tamar.

Just down-river from here the National Trust plans to create a greater area of reed-bed by reflooding approximately 16 hectares of farmland, which was taken from the river by the formation of retaining banks some time in the nineteenth century. Though this plan has been supported by the Environment Agency, Natural England and the RSPB, there has been some local resistance. There is every likelihood that at some time in the near future this scheme will get the go-ahead, and this will create a significant improvement in the biodiversity of the area, offering a potential breeding site to birds such as marsh harrier and bittern. It will also surely help to prevent flooding by re-opening the floodplain to the river's disposal.

The path from the quay to Cotehele Mill follows a small river in the Morden Valley. Here it may be possible to see dipper and grey wagtail – our two classic riparian birds. Nearer the mill there is a damp meadow with cuckoo flower in spring. This is a good spot for dragonflies and butterflies in summer.

Above: Cotehele is probably the best place in Cornwall to see autumnal colour.
Right: Mistletoe grows in the orchard at Cotehele.

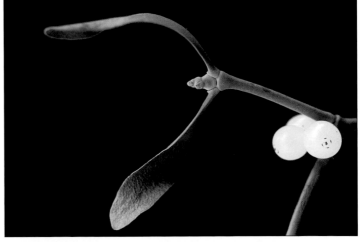

Walking north from the quay along the River Tamar, we have woodland to the left and tidal river to the right. One of the most common bird sounds here is that of the nuthatch, but unusually its competition might come from a curlew. The ground flora of the woodland is particularly good for wood anemones, but also includes bluebells, lesser celandine and wood sorrel. Around the woodland of the estate as little intervention as possible is made by the Trust

The avocet graces the River Tamar mostly just to the south of Cotehele.

staff. However, there is an ongoing battle against the invasive species of rhododendron and laurel which are being removed. The Trust's policy on managing woodland is to fell dangerous trees, but generally wood is now left to rot *in situ*, providing a home for insects and fungi.

The ruined mines of the Danescombe Valley are home to roosting bats. Probably the most significant bats in the area are the greater and lesser horseshoes. Great efforts are being made to protect these species in the Tamar AONB, not only by protecting their roost sites, but also through direct communication with all the farmers in the area.

The formal gardens offer an interesting mix of native and non-native plants. The orchard at Cotehele is the best place in Cornwall to see mistletoe. It grows on relatively low branches of the apple trees, allowing closer inspection than is usually possible of this parasitic species. There is a splendid showing of snakeshead fritillaries close to the house. No doubt these were originally planted here, but there are very few places left where they were not. The south-

Snakeshead fritillaries are a feature of the gardens in spring.

through water at its surface for tiny crustacea. Their black and white plumage makes them instantly identifiable, but they are not a common sight in Cornwall; in fact, you would be very lucky to see one anywhere other than in East Cornwall. They nest primarily in the east of England, and come to the West Country for the winter. Most head for the Exe Estuary, but some always come to the Tamar. If you don't see them here, then a drive to the village of Cargreen, a few miles to the south, should do the trick.

facing slope of the small valley leading down from the house towards the Tamar is a great spot for a mass of primroses and dog violets, growing underneath young magnolias.

A special mention must be made of the daffodils of Cotehele, because the gardeners here are working to save the ancient breeds of daffodil found around the estate. During the Second World War, when land was at a premium, some people planted daffodil bulbs in the hedgerows to earn a little extra cash from ground that would have been of no use for growing vegetables. Many of these daffodils were unusual strains, and the search is now on to find and save representatives of each type.

I have spoken relatively little of the tidal river at Cotehele, though it is possible that, in addition to seeing here the variety of waders that can be seen in other parts of the county, you might encounter an avocet. These unusual waders have an upturned bill, suited to their feeding technique, which is to sift

LOOK OUT FOR

February–April: Best time for listening to and watching nuthatches, treecreepers and three species of woodpecker – great spotted, green and lesser spotted. Daffodils are in bloom.

April–May: Spring flowers in the woods include bluebell, wood anemone and wood sorrel. In the gardens look out for spectacular displays of snakeshead fritillaries and primroses.

May–August: Spotted flycatchers hunt in woodland clearings, reed and sedge warblers nest in the reeds alongside the Tamar. Barn owls hunt over open areas of land, using nest boxes provided by the estate staff. At least four species of bat have been recorded, including the greater and lesser horseshoes, which roost in the old mine adits.

July–August: Silver-washed fritillary.

October–November: The autumn colour here is probably the best in Cornwall.

December: Best time for mistletoe in the orchard.

November–February: Waders on the creek include redshank, curlew and avocet.

All year: Roe deer in the woods. Maidenhair fern and maidenhair spleenwort grow on the lime-kilns at the quay. Reed bunting in the reeds; along the Morden Valley there are grey wagtails and dippers.

location	Private garden
map	*Explorer* 108; *Landranger* 201
directions to start point	By road: Take A374 from Antony towards Torpoint; turn L approx 1 ml before Torpoint, signed Antony House & Antony Woodland Garden. Continue on this minor road past Antony House (NT). Park where indicated
starting point	SX 416 567
size	approx 30 ha/approx 75 a
length	Approx 3 ml
suggested time	4 hours
conditions	Good quality footpaths
habitats	Woodland, pond, garden, estuary, meadow
interest	Formal gardens: around SX 415 567 Woodland gardens: around SX 423 568
designation	AONB
owner	Carew Pole Trust
open	1 March–31 October, 11 am to 5 pm (not Mondays, Fridays)
entry	Charge
enquiries	T: 01752 814 210 (CPT)
facilities	Torpoint
facilities	

Antony Woodland Garden

Wildlife isn't always attracted to areas that we would describe as beautiful, but when it is we can count ourselves very fortunate. Antony Woodland Garden near Torpoint is just such a place. Despite its being home to a national collection of *Camellia japonica*, and all that might be implied about its formality, this woodland garden is a place of rare natural as well as semi-natural delights.

The Carew Pole family have lived at Antony since 1432. The current house, in which they still live, was built in the early eighteenth century, and up until then the gardens were very much restricted to an area close to the house. During the latter part of the eighteenth century the Rt. Hon. Reginald Carew Pole had a larger vision for the gardens, and employed the landscape gardener Humphry Repton to transform the land between the house and the River Lynher.

The main focus of their efforts was the planting of a huge number of trees in such a way as to lead the eye towards the river from the house, using a series of glades. Successive generations of the family have further enhanced the appearance of the gardens by planting more trees, as well as many types of garden shrubs, including rhododendrons, azaleas, magnolias and camellias. Camellias were a particular favourite, and there are currently over 400 different varieties here. The woodland gardens are now essentially separated from the house, since the National Trust owns the house and its immediate surroundings, and the woodland gardens, bordering the river, are managed by the Carew Pole Garden Trust, which is a charity.

A path meanders through Antony Woodland Garden.

Left: Tawny owls live in the old trees around the garden.
Top: The green woodpecker can be seen at Antony.
Above: Coal tits are most likely to be seen in the evergreen trees.

The woodland gardens are split into two parts. To the west of the road leading down to Jupiter Point is

Above: Wild garlic carpets the ground at Antony.
Right: Orange tip butterflies emerge at the same time as bluebells.

the more formal area, which includes the camellias, magnolias and rhododendrons. To the east of the road is an area of natural woodland and meadow. Both sections are beautiful in their own right, but the formal gardens are probably the more attractive in early spring (March and April), whereas the wooded section comes into its own with the emergence of the bluebells and wild garlic in late April.

The fact that many of the trees here were planted nearly three centuries ago hints at the value which they now provide for our native wildlife. Large, old trees with gnarled trunks provide fissures, cracks and holes for birds to nest. As the holes are made bigger through time we see a change in their patronage – from tits to woodpeckers, and eventually owls. Even in the middle of the day it is sometimes possible to locate tawny owls, since they are often roused from their sleep by a noisy blackbird, concerned for either its own well-being or that of its young. The wheezy calls of the tawny owl – nothing like the 'twit-twoo'

which it often makes as darkness falls – are uttered in annoyance at being disturbed by this irritating upstart, and as its response grows to a climax the owl may break cover to find a new roost for the day.

All around is evidence of woodpeckers, of which there are three species here. The great spotted woodpeckers give away their presence readily with loud chick-chick calls, and often come to the garden by the gatehouse cottage to feed from the peanut feeders.

Looking across the River Lynher from the woodland.

Even louder are the green woodpeckers which nest in the bigger, older, more decayed trees. Their maniacal laughter, or yaffle, is always obvious in places such as this, where short grass and old trees live alongside each other. The third species, the lesser spotted woodpecker, is a small and quiet bird living high up in the branches of mature trees. The best chance of finding one of these diminutive birds is to visit in early spring, and to listen for its drumming, which is lighter in weight than the sound produced by the much larger great spotted woodpecker.

As well as the three species of woodpecker, there are numerous nuthatches and treecreepers, all clambering around on the trunks of the wonderful trees of this garden. Such is the activity among the trees that it is quite possible to spend an entire visit wandering around looking up!

Therein lies a quandary, because in late April and early May it is difficult to take your eyes off the ground since, unlike many more formal gardens around the county, Antony encourages, and indeed celebrates, our native woodland flowers. The simple strategy of leaving areas of grassland unmown through the spring and summer, with the exception of pathways, is enough to ensure that wildflowers flourish. The result of two or three centuries of unhindered growth is a carpet – and I use the word literally – of bluebells and wild garlic. Nowhere else can I recall seeing such a mix of these two species. What a spectacle it is to see so much luxuriant and colourful growth around the base of such a wide variety of trees and shrubs.

One flower which grows well here in the damper meadows is the cuckoo flower, or lady's smock. Where you see cuckoo flower you have every chance of seeing an orange tip butterfly. Not only do they both occur at the same time, but also the leaves of the cuckoo flower are food for the butterfly's caterpillar.

Swathes of bluebells sweep down to the river's edge, where there are plenty of benches on which to sit and enjoy the view while picking out a few species typical of this very special environment. In winter curlew, redshank and oystercatcher are numerous.

Foxes are common at Antony.

the strengths in both. The dense thickets of rhododendron are obviously popular with nesting warblers, particularly blackcaps, which presumably feel safe while singing from beneath their dark foliage. A pair of ravens has nested for many years at the top of a very tall fir tree in the middle of the tended garden. Many other birds, such as mistle thrush and jay (throughout the year), and spotted flycatcher (in the summer), make their home in the formal gardens. Other highlights include nesting mallard and Canada geese on the ponds – one of which is surrounded by bulrushes and irises. There are also deer in the area – both roe and fallow – their footprints or slots can be seen in the muddier paths. Other mammals much in evidence include foxes and badgers.

It seems an irony that our natural history should be more varied in an environment which has been so heavily manipulated by our hand, but at Antony Woodland Garden the manipulation has created a diversity and richness of habitat that is rare.

A plentiful supply of fish means that there is always the chance of seeing a little egret, grey heron or even kingfisher. On Beggar's Island cormorants stand drying their wings and digesting their latest catch, with only gulls for company. Closer to shore, plodding around on the exposed mud, are one or two shelducks, which presumably nest in the woodland.

It is tempting to think that our native birds would favour the natural woodland in preference to the more manicured gardens, but that doesn't seem to be the case. Where non-native plants are mixed with natives, birds seem to be able to take advantage of

---

LOOK OUT FOR

March–May: The formal gardens are at their best for species such as magnolia and camellia.

April–May: Flowers include bluebells, wild garlic, early purple orchid, bugle, cuckoo flower and lords and ladies. Look for orange tip butterflies around the cuckoo flowers.

Summer: Migrant breeding birds include garden warbler, blackcap, willow warbler, swallow and spotted flycatcher.

August–October: Look out for waders on the estuary, and fungi in the woods.

All year: Raven, mistle thrush, tawny owl, lesser spotted woodpecker, great spotted woodpecker, green woodpecker, nuthatch, treecreeper, grey heron, little egret, jay, sparrowhawk, shelduck and cormorant.

site number

type of location

map

directions to
start point

starting point

length

recommended time

conditions

habitats

points of interest

landscape designation

owner

open

entry

enquiries

site facilities

40

Country park

Explorer 108; *Landranger* 201

By road: From Trerulefoot round-about on A38, take A374 to Mount Edgcumbe. Turn R on B3247 to Crafthole, and L in village. Follow signs to Kingsand, then Rame Head. Park by Lookout station

Rame Head car-park SX 422 487; other car-parks Kingsand SX 432 503; Penlee Battery SX 437 491; many near Mount Edgcumbe House

12 ml (or separate into two shorter walks)

6 hours

Typical coast path

Coast, cliff, meadow, woodland, parkland, garden

Penlee Battery (CWT reserve): SX 439 491; Grotto: SX 442 488; Mount Edgcumbe House and Gardens: SX 453 527

AONB

CCC and Plymouth City Council

Estate: All year

Free (charge for gardens)

T: 01752 822 236 (Mount Edgcumbe); W: www.mountedgcumbe.gov.uk

Note: Limited wheelchair access around house and gardens

Mount Edgcumbe and Rame Head

Rame Head, the start of my suggested walk along the coast path to Mount Edgcumbe, can be a wild and windy place. The wind can gain greater velocity as it funnels through the dip between the Coastguard lookout and the ruined chapel on top of the promontory from where the Spanish Armada was first spotted. In such conditions it is clear that any birds here have to be hardened and at the peak of condition. Those that are know exactly how to handle a breeze!

The kestrels here are in their element: they don't need wind in order to hover, but they can cope with it well enough. They always hover with their heads facing into the wind, and like to use the upward blast of air created by a slope where they can get added lift. Their skill seems all the more astonishing in a gale, when through twists and turns of tail and wing they manage to keep their head static. It is stabilizing their head that matters most of all, because only with a steady eye will they have a chance of picking out field voles among the longer grass of the headland.

The nimble little kestrels are often joined here by the much larger buzzard. Give a buzzard a stiff breeze and it will do its best to match the kestrel – but they most definitely have not yet mastered the art of hovering in still air. If the breeze is steady, a buzzard can hover for a few seconds, but as soon as the wind changes force or direction it will lose it. The preferred hunting technique for a buzzard is to watch for prey while sitting on a perch such as a telegraph pole or tall tree, but here there is no such luxury.

Also present here is a pair of ravens; their flight is somewhat nonchalant and seemingly unaffected

The ruined chapel at Rame Head.

The kestrel is the only bird of prey that can truly hover.

by the wind, but in late winter the raven adds a little spice to its behaviour as pairs begin to establish bonds in readiness for nesting. Nesting is carried out early in the year, so that the young are born when there is plenty of carrion available. In an attempt to impress each other, the ravens fly high in the sky and tumble in front of each other; often one bird will be on the ground while the other shows off. Another strategy employed by the male is to bring his partner a tasty piece of carrion to seduce her. It is rare to get close to a raven, but getting close isn't necessary to appreciate their huge size and strength. The only bird that is even superficially similar to the raven is the carrion crow, but the raven's superior size and croaking call should be sufficient to identify it in most circumstances.

The one other bird at Rame Head which can be guaranteed to set the pulse racing is the peregrine falcon. These incredibly strong, barrel-breasted hunters cut through the air of the turbulent headland as if it were motionless. Starting from a height, the peregrine can stoop at great speeds (a captive bird has been recorded to stoop at approximately 200 miles per hour!), and it is this skill, combined with the element of surprise, which the bird uses to catch other birds in flight.

Pairs of peregrine falcons like to look out for one another, and they are happy to join together to see off any opposition, so when a buzzard approaches they will take it in turns to assault it. The buzzard is ridiculously ill-equipped for an airborne fight with a

Left: The peregrine is the fastest bird on the planet.
Right: Ravens are carrion eaters.

This fallow buck has adorned himself with bracken to make himself look impressive.

peregrine, let alone two, and has no choice but to beat a hasty retreat. It is a little surprising that peregrines bother chasing a buzzard, but maybe they think it might scare off their intended prey.

Walking north from the headland, things begin to mellow a little. A short distance along the path, and a small detour off it, is the Cornwall Wildlife Trust reserve at Penlee Battery. This reserve is at its most interesting in early summer, since it is home to a wide range of grassland flowers, including the pretty bee orchid which flowers in mid-June. As with much of the coast around here, the vegetation is kept in check by a herd of Dartmoor ponies. They are kept here not only to benefit the environment, but also for breeding purposes: an attempt is being made to maintain the purity of the Dartmoor pony through selective breeding.

Returning to the coast path and rounding the bend by the rather eccentric grotto – an eighteenth-century modified cave used as a watch point – a different, and softer, appearance is created by woodland, not all of which comprises native species. Along the track, known as the Earl's Drive, are laurels and holm oaks, providing year-round greenery. The ground beneath them is quite barren, but in the deciduous sections of the wood, bluebells, wild garlic and dog's mercury are all common.

A short distance beyond the picturesque villages of Cawsand and Kingsand is the landscaped park-land of Mount Edgcumbe. The land around here has been the subject of human activity for millennia. The oldest feature we are aware of is a Bronze Age barrow, but there are other influences, such as those of the Vikings.

Approaching the formal part of the estate around the house of Mount Edgcumbe, the first obvious sign of grandeur is the deer park. Fallow deer were first introduced here in the time of Henry VIII, in around 1515. They have lived here ever since, becoming ever wilder as they strayed on to the surrounding

Common broomrape can be found at Penlee Battery.

The parkland surrounding the formal gardens is a rare habitat in Cornwall. The mixture of short grass and mature trees is loved by two birds in particular: the green woodpecker and the mistle thrush, both of which have an undulating flight and a distinctive call. In the formal gardens there are also breeding blackcaps, jays, great spotted and lesser spotted woodpeckers.

The walk from Rame Head is quite a long one, particularly if you have to walk back again, but access around the estate is almost unlimited, so there is plenty of potential for creating walks in different parts of the estate. It can get busy here at weekends, particularly around the house and gardens, so a visit on a weekday, and possibly early in the morning would be best to see wildlife.

land. Today the deer are not so much fenced in on the estate as fenced out of the formal gardens. Fallow deer are quite variable in colour, but look out for the attractive spotted coats of the majority of deer, and the characteristic palm-shaped antlers of the mature stags.

LOOK OUT FOR

April–May: Flowers along the coast include dog violet, lesser celandine, sea campion, thrift, kidney vetch, and bird's-foot trefoil. Slightly less common are shore dock and slender bird's-foot trefoil. This is a good time to see fallow deer as they get together in herds.

June: The CWT reserve is good for wild flowers in summer, including bee orchid, yellow bartsia, wild basil, and the parasitic species common broomrape.

August–September: Autumn lady's tresses grow on the lawn in front of the house.

September–October: The headland is attractive to migrant birds, so any woodland or scrub could hold warblers and finches. The more exposed parts might play host to wheatears, pipits, buntings and larks.

All year: Ravens nest on the coast, and a good range of breeding birds of prey around the country park include sparrowhawk, buzzard, peregrine, kestrel, tawny and barn owls.

Year Planner

Below are some of the best places to go by month. This does not mean that other places are not worth visiting then. Sites are listed by number.

January
2   Bude Canal
5   Camel Estuary
10 Hayle Estuary
11 St Ives
19 Marazion Marsh
21 Loe Pool
27 Tresillian River
40 Mount Edgcumbe and Rame Head

February
2   Bude Canal
5   Camel Estuary
10 Hayle Estuary
11 St Ives
19 Marazion Marsh
21 Loe Pool
27 Tresillian River
38 Cotehele
40 Mount Edgcumbe and Rame Head

March
25 Kennall Vale
27 Tresillian River
28 Lost Gardens of Heligan
32 Lanhydrock
36 Kit Hill
38 Cotehele
39 Antony Woodland Garden
40 Mount Edgcumbe and Rame Head

April
1   Welcombe and Marsland
20 Godolphin
25 Kennall Vale
28 Lost Gardens of Heligan
29 Luxulyan Valley
32 Lanhydrock
33 Cabilla and Redrice
34 Kilminorth Woods
38 Cotehele
39 Antony Woodland Garden

May
1   Welcombe and Marsland
3   Boscastle
6   West Pentire
15 St Mary's
16 Tresco
17 St Martin's
20 Godolphin
22 Kynance to Lizard
25 Kennall Vale
28 Heligan
29 Luxulyan Valley
30 Goss Moor
31 Breney Common
32 Lanhydrock
33 Cabilla and Redrice
34 Kilminorth Woods
39 Antony Woodland Garden

June
2   Bude Canal
3   Boscastle
4   Polzeath
6   West Pentire
7   Penhale Sands
9   Godrevy to Upton Towans
12 Bosigran and Gurnard's Head
14 Boscregan Farm
15 St Mary's
16 Tresco
17 St Martin's
22 Kynance to Lizard
24 Goonhilly Downs
26 Bissoe Valley
28 Lost Gardens of Heligan
30 Goss Moor

July
2   Bude Canal
4   Polzeath
6   West Pentire
7   Penhale Sands
9   Godrevy to Upton Towans
14 Boscregan Farm
23 Windmill Farm
26 Bissoe Valley
31 Breney Common

August
4   Polzeath
11 St Ives
18 Porthgwarra
19 Marazion Marsh
21 Loe Pool
23 Windmill Farm
24 Goonhilly Downs
26 Bissoe Valley

September
10 Hayle Estuary
11 St Ives
13 Cot Valley
15 St Mary's
16 Tresco
17 St Martin's
18 Porthgwarra
19 Marazion Marsh
22 Kynance to Lizard
24 Goonhilly Downs
27 Tresillian River
33 Cabilla and Redrice

October
8   Tehidy Country Park
10 Hayle Estuary
13 Cot Valley
15 St Mary's
16 Tresco
17 St Martin's
18 Porthgwarra

31 Breney Common
36 Kit Hill
37 Sylvia's Meadow

22 Kynance to Lizard
33 Cabilla and Redrice
35 Golitha Falls

November
5   Camel Estuary
8   Tehidy Country Park
10 Hayle Estuary
19 Marazion Marsh
29 Luxulyan Valley
35 Golitha Falls
38 Cotehele

December
5   Camel Estuary
10 Hayle Estuary
19 Marazion Marsh
21 Loe Pool
27 Tresillian River
38 Cotehele

Location Planner

Below are listed some of the best months to go to each place. This does not mean that a site is not worth visiting in other months. Sites are listed by name.

Antony Woodland Garden, 39: Mar, Apr, May

Bissoe Valley, 26: Jun, Jul, Aug

Boscastle, 3: May, Jun

Boscregan Farm, 14: Jun, Jul

Bosigran and Gurnard's Head, 12: Jun

Breney Common: 31, May, Jun, Jul

Bude Canal, 2: Jan, Feb, Jun, Jul

Cabilla and Redrice, 33: Apr, May, Sep, Oct

Camel Estuary, 5: Jan, Feb, Nov, Dec

Cot Valley, 13: Sep, Oct

Cotehele, 38: Feb, Mar, Apr, Nov, Dec

Godolphin, 20: Apr, May

Godrevy to Upton Towans, 9: Jun, Jul

Golitha Falls, 35: Oct, Nov

Goonhilly Downs, 24: Jun, Aug, Sep

Goss Moor, 30: May, Jun

Hayle Estuary, 10: Jan, Feb, Sep, Oct, Nov, Dec

Kennall Vale, 25. Mar, Apr, May

Kilminorth Woods: 34, Apr, May

Kit Hill, 36: Mar, Jun

Kynance to Lizard, 22: May, Jun, Sep, Oct

Lanhydrock Estate, 32: Mar, Apr, May

Loe Pool, 21: Jan, Feb, Aug, Dec

Lost Gardens of Heligan, 28: Mar, Apr, May, Jun

Luxulyan Valley, 29: Apr, May, Nov

Marazion Marsh, 19: Jan, Feb, Aug, Sep, Nov, Dec

Mount Edgcumbe and Rame Head, 40: Jan, Feb, Mar

Penhale Sands, 7: Jun, Jul

Polzeath, 4: Jun, Jul, Aug

Porthgwarra, 18: Aug, Sep, Oct

St Ives, 11: Jan, Feb, Aug, Sep

St Martin's, 17: May, Jun, Sep, Oct

St Mary's, 15: May, Jun, Sep, Oct

Sylvia's Meadow: 37, Jun

Tehidy Country Park, 8: Oct, Nov

Tresco, 16: May, Jun, Sep, Oct

Tresillian River, 27: Jan, Feb, Mar, Sep, Dec

Welcombe and Marsland, 1: Apr, May

West Pentire, 6: May, Jun, Jul

Windmill Farm, 23: Jul, Aug

Organizations and Groups

The following are the owners or managers of the sites in the text. Those asterisked are seeking members or friends.

Caradon District Council, Luxstowe House, Liskeard PL14 3DZ. T: 01579 341 000; W: www.caradon.gov.uk

Carew Pole Trust, Antony House, Torpoint PL11 2QA. T: 01752 814 210

*Cornwall Bird-Watching & Preservation Society, current secretary: Darrell Clegg, T: 01752 844 775; E: Darrell@bluetail.fsnet.co.uk

Cornwall County Council, Natural Environment Service, St Clement Building, Old County Hall, Truro TR1 3AY. T: 01872 222 000; W: www.cornwall.gov.uk

*Cornwall Wildlife Trust, Five Acres, Allet, nr Truro TR4 9DJ. T: 01872 273 939; W: www.cornwallwildlifetrust.org.uk

Isles of Scilly Wildlife Trust, Carn Thomas, St Mary's, Isles of Scilly TR21 0PT. T: 01720 422 153; W: www.ios-wildlifetrust.org.uk

*The Lost Gardens of Heligan, Pentewan, St Austell PL26 6EN. T: 01726 845 100; W: www.heligan.com

*National Trust, Cornwall Office, Lanhydrock, Bodmin PL30 4DE. T: 01208 742 81; W: www.nationaltrust.org.uk

Natural England, Cornwall & Isles of Scilly Team, Trevint House, Strangways Villas, Truro TR1 2PA. T: 01872 265 710, head office 01733 455 000; W: www.naturalengland.org.uk

North Cornwall District Council, Coast & Countryside Service, North Cornwall District Council, 3/5 Barn Lane, Bodmin PL31 1LZ. T: 01208 265 644; W: www.ncdc.gov.uk

*Royal Society for the Protection of Birds, The RSPB South West Regional Office, Keble House, Southernhay Gardens, Exeter EX1 1NT. T: 01392 432 691; W: www.rspb.org.uk

Field Craft

- **Dusk and dawn** are the best times for watching birds and animals.
- Be **quiet** and walk steadily.
- The most important consideration when trying to get a good view of birds or shy animals is how they sense you. Creatures with good eyesight will see you from a long way away if you wear bright clothes and stand on a bank in the open – so don't. Choose your clothes sensibly – **dark clothes** are best, and some waterproofs are much quieter than others. Always try to use surrounding vegetation to mask your presence; don't just consider what is between you and the target of your attention, but also what is behind you. If you wear dark clothes and stand in front of dark trees you won't be very obvious, but if you stand on a bank so that you can be seen against the sky, you will scare everything off. Don't be afraid to get down low if it is the only way to avoid breaking the horizon. Finally, your scent can alert an animal to your presence. Some mammals, such as otters, badgers and deer, have a very good sense of smell, so try to stay down-wind of these animals.
- **Be aware** of what is going on around you, and respond accordingly.
- **Use all your senses**. Eyesight is important in our enjoyment of wildlife, but we tend to over-depend on this sense. Hearing is the most useful sense in locating wildlife, so walk quietly. Once you find something of interest, watching it is important and rewarding, but there is no substitute for touching a moss; smelling an otter spraint, or listening to a grasshopper warbler.
- Check **tide times** if you are visiting an estuary, or are rock-pooling. For rock-pooling the tide needs to be as far out as possible, but don't be caught out by the tide rising. For watching birds at an estuary, the tide should be coming in; a couple of hours before high tide is a good time to start.
- Carry a **notepad and pencil**: it is interesting to build up a personal diary. Records of unusual species should be sent to the Cornwall Wildlife Trust's record centre. Facts you should record for submission include: date; time; species; number seen; map reference, and any notes or photographs that might verify your record.
- **Binoculars** are almost always important to a wildlife-watcher. When buying binoculars, consider their magnification and size. Binoculars are given a rating including two numbers: for example 8 x 30. The first number is their magnification, and the second is the diameter of their objective lens (the lens at the far end) in millimetres. Many people think that the bigger the magnification the better, but this simply is not true. When a pair of binoculars becomes too powerful, it is impossible to hold steady. I favour a magnification of 8x, but anywhere between 7x and 10x should be fine. The objective lens should be as big as you are prepared to carry around – the bigger the lens the brighter the image. Compact binoculars have a small objective lens of say 20–24 mm, but their image can look quite dull. If you need to use a small pair, choose a correspondingly small magnification: 7 x 24 will be good, but 10 x 20 will not. If you are looking for something of an intermediate size then 8 x 30 is a useful configuration (this is my choice), and if you are prepared to use something bigger then 10 x 40 will give a good image. Also consider whether you will use your binoculars with spectacles – some have fold-down rubber eye cups for use with spectacles. Finally, price – generally the higher the price the better the optics and build quality. Try a range of different binoculars, and find a pair you feel comfortable with.

Country Codes

In the countryside

- Leave gates as you find them.
- Keep dogs under control; clean up after them.
- Do not pick flowers or uproot plants.
- Do not leave litter.
- Take care not to start a fire.
- Keep to rights of way.
- Drive carefully on country roads.
- Cyclists must keep to bridleways and specially designed tracks.

At the seashore

- Do not take live specimens away from the beach; always leave live animals where you find them.
- If you look under rocks, always replace them, carefully, where they were.
- Do not remove seaweed from rocks.
- Only take shells if you are sure they are empty.
- Many seashells sold in shops had animals living inside them when they were collected. Examine your conscience before buying them.
- Check the tide times and keep an eye on the sea.

Birds' nesting

Whenever you come close to the nests of breeding birds there is a danger that your presence will cause them to desert their nests. If ever you notice that birds are making themselves obvious to you – through repeated mobbing, feigning injury or making excessive noise – then you should leave the area. Watch them from a safe distance, but use their behaviour to allow them to dictate that distance.

Wildlife and the law

The Wildlife and Countryside Act 1981 details the protection of species of animals and plants in Britain. Details are on the website **www.naturenet.net**.

Recommended Reading

Field guides

Brooks, S., Lewington, R., 1997, *Field Guide to the Dragonflies and Damselflies of Great Britain and Ireland*. Milton on Stour: British Wildlife Publishing

Chinery, M., 1998, *Butterflies of Britain and Europe*. Glasgow: Collins

Chinery, M., 1993, *Collins Guide to the Insects of Britain and Western Europe*. Glasgow: Collins

Fitter, R., Fitter, A. and Blamey. M., 1996, *Wild Flowers of Britain and Northern Europe*. Glasgow: Collins

Jonsson, L., 1992, *The Birds of Europe: With North Africa and the Middle East*. London: Christopher Helm

Lang, D., 2004, *Britain's Orchids*. Old Basing: WILDGuides

Phillips, R., Shearer, L., Reid, D. (ed.), 1981, *Mushrooms and Other Fungi of Great Britain and Europe*. London: Pan

Reader's Digest, 2001, *Field Guide to the Trees and Shrubs of Britain* (Nature Lover's Library). London: Reader's Digest

Sterry, P., 1997, *Collins Complete British Wildlife: Photographic*. Glasgow: Collins

Waring, P., Townsend, M., Lewington, R., 2003, *Field Guide to the Moths of Great Britain and Ireland*. Milton on Stour: British Wildlife Publishing

Further reading

Cornwall Wildlife Trust: Nature Reserves Handbook (Environmental Records Centre for Cornwall & the Isles of Scilly, 2003).

The National Trust's Coast of Cornwall leaflets.

Norman, D., Tucker, V., Harrison, P., 1991, *Where to Watch Birds in Devon and Cornwall*. London: Christopher Helm.

For further wildlife locations around the county, see David Chapman's series of articles 'Wild About Cornwall' in the magazine *Cornwall Today*.

Species Index